Supernatural Keys to the Higher Dimension

Unlocking the Treasure in the Heavenly Realm

Suri Devaraj

Copyright © 2011 by Suri Devaraj

Supernatural Keys to the Higher Dimension
Unlocking the Treasure in the Heavenly Realm
by Suri Devaraj

Printed in the United States of America

ISBN 9781619047754

All rights reserved solely by the author. The author guarantees all contents are original and do not infringe upon the legal rights of any other person or work. No part of this book may be reproduced in any form without the permission of the author. The views expressed in this book are not necessarily those of the publisher.

Unless otherwise indicated, Bible quotations are taken from The Holy Bible; The King James Version; The NEW AMERICAN STANDARD BIBLE®. Copyright © 1960, 1962, 1963, 1971, 1972, 1973, 1975, 1977, 1995 by The Lockman Foundation; and The Holy Bible, English Standard Version. Copyright © 2001 by Crossway Bibles, a division of Good News Publishers. Used by permission.

www.xulonpress.com

Acknowledgments

First of all I would like to thank God for helping me write this book. He is the one who gave me the anointing and power to see in the spiritual realm. I praise Him for giving me many supernatural visitations as well as outstanding healings and miracles.

I would like to honor my parents, the late Dr. Sathyanand and Sarojini Sathyanand. God used my dad to bring revival in our state of Karnataka, South India. He was well known among many people and a man of prayer. His life of prayer and faith were a huge inspiration to me. My mom is another strong person in my life who is the backbone of prayer. She is over eighty years old and still spends hours with God each day.

I would also like to acknowledge my four special sisters, Sheela, Ruth, Meena, and Lalitha. They are gems. They have always stood with me in prayer and believed for great things. They pray day and night, whenever it is needed. I can never forget their support. They are a great blessing to me.

My brothers, Samuel and Stephen, are also a great encouragement to me. They always help my family and I with many practical things. My nephews, Ranju and John, are always there to help when I need them.

I also thank God for my brothers-in-law: Victor Kantharaj, Deva Prasad, and Sunil Kirby. I'm also thankful for my cousins: David and Dr. Daniel.

I want to thank my wife, Tammy, who took a lot of time with me in helping to write this book. Though she is busy with the administration of our ministry and taking care of our three kids, she sacrificed a lot of her sleep to help me to write this book in order for it to be a blessing to many. She is very busy doing all the things Proverbs 31 speaks about. I love her and my three kids, Abri, Micah, and Andrew, who are a big inspiration for me to go further.

I would also like to say thank you to Becky Kantharaj, my niece, who helped with this book too. I also want to thank my special friends who prayed and encouraged me to write this book as well as who have stood with me and encouraged me in the ministry: Jan Gerrit Otterpohl, Ajay Rajani, Murugan Subramanian, and Ben Mathew.

A special thanks to Pastor Dave Roberson, who is a wonderful pastor and prophet. He has been such a powerful blessing in my life. His prophetic words have guided me many times because they came straight from God through him. I thank God for his life.

I also thank God for the men of God in Karnataka, South India: Bro. S.R. Manohar, Rev. Prabhakar Ayya, Bro. Ram Babu, and many others.

Dedication

I would like to dedicate this book to my parents, the late Dr. Sathyanand and Sarojini Sathyanand, who served God for many years and stood for the truth.

Also, to all the men and women of God who are preaching and teaching the gospel—risking their lives for Jesus. Their lives are an inspiration to me.

Endorsements

I have had the privilege to meet Rev. Suri Devaraj a couple of times in Sweden. From the first time I saw him I got the impression that this is one of the rare prayer warriors who will prevail with God until the victory is won. He has a genuine burden for the work of God and his ministry has been a great blessing to many people in Sweden. The few times we have been able to fellowship have been sweet moments, when God's presence has been very real. Out of his close relationship to the Lord and many years of ministry he is now sharing precious truths from the word of God and I'm sure that this book will be a great blessing to all those who will read it.

— Rev. Curt Johansson

Director Bethel Faith Ministries

Bollnäs, Sweden

(Established 1,500 churches in Kenya, Tanzania, Uganda, Rwanda, and the Congo. Established five hundred churches in the nation of India.)

As pastors of a local church just north of London, we have known Suri as a good friend for fifteen years. Suri visits Europe regularly, and we love to spend time with him as a man who chases after God, hears His voice, sees Him move in others' lives and brings His presence wherever he goes.

— Pastors Mike & Heather Dyce
City Church Hatfield, England

I am eager to know how to stay in the presence of God, which is the key for all the blessings in Christ Jesus. Bro. Suri's book is the culmination of all the authors who have authored on the supernatural living, plus bonus of his experience in the same realm! It is my privilege and honor to know Bro. Suri from his teen years. I thank the Lord, who brought me in touch with him in our journey. The hunger he has for God reminds me of the hunger of the Sons of Korah in Psalm 42:1-2. It is easy to move with him as his simplicity of devotion to Christ is transparent. Bro. Suri is an encouragement to me. I strongly recommend God's people to get hold of this book on the supernatural life for yourself and give it as a gift to others! As you water others, you shall be watered!

— E.D. Chelladurai
Senior Pastor
Good Shepherd Community Church Bangalore, India

Pastor Suri has been a most welcome visitor to our church where his ministry has had a lasting impact on a good number of people. We praise God for him and recognize his teaching comes with a wealth of experience across the world where he has been used by God in transforming many lives.

— Canon Tony Hurle
St. Paul's Church, St. Albans, England

As I've pastored Suri Devaraj, I have found him to be man who has an undying passion to reach the lost for Christ and a heart to help believers walk in the fullness of God's love and provision. Suri desires to see believers experience the glory of God where needs are met and intimacy with the Father is restored.

— Pastor Gary Mitrik
Senior Pastor, Greater Works Outreach

It was a joy to work and grow with Suri as he is a bubbling man, full of anointing. Especially when he was studying in the college, he was such an inspiration for us to pray. He loves the Lord passionately. He has grown deep in the experiences with the Holy Spirit, which always stir us up to get closer to the Lord like Suri does because we know his experiences are genuine. Whatever he writes, it is with deep experiential knowledge and yet he sticks with the Word of God. It gives me joy to recommend this book to anyone who wants to grow strong and deep in the knowledge of God.

— Pastor Sunil Mahade
Senior Pastor, El-Shaddai Worship Center
Hubli, India

Table of Contents

Introduction xvii

Chapter 1: Man Is A Spirit Being 21
Chapter 2: What Does Your Spirit Look Like? 24
Chapter 3: Taking Care Of Your Inner Man 29
Chapter 4: Taking Away The Veil 34
Chapter 5: Losing Your Identity (Fear) 39
Chapter 6: Controlled By The Wrong Spirit 49
Chapter 7: Breaking Strongholds From Your Mind 57
Chapter 8: The Discerning Of Spirits 59
Chapter 9: Undoing All The Wrong Things 98
Chapter 10: Extraordinary Power From
           Above To Overcome 101
Chapter 11: Righteousness 109
Chapter 12: Use God's Word As A Promise 112

xv

Chapter 13: Reading And Meditating 122
Chapter 14: What You See Can Be Yours 127
Chapter 15: Faith...134
Chapter 16: Difference Between Faith And Senses 156
Chapter 17: The Power Of Praise And Worship 159
Chapter 18: The Power Of The Holy Spirit 166
Chapter 19: Are You Thirsty? 172
Chapter 20: The Language That Unlocks
 The Heavenly Realm 183
Chapter 21: The Glory Of God 229
Chapter 22: Transported..232

Conclusion 245

Introduction

After I was filled with the Holy Spirit, God gave me a passion to be in His presence. This passion helped me read, meditate, and learn from His Word as well. I started my ministry by spending many hours with Him each and every day, which connected me to the heavenly realm. God began to download His wisdom and knowledge into me.

As I spent more time in His presence, the Lord began visiting me in many different ways. He would often transport me to different nations and to various people, mainly to pray for their healing and deliverance. His glory has been tangibly real to me since being filled with His Spirit.

He has given me some powerful, supernatural keys, which have helped thousands of people around the world as I've shared them. In this book you will see how you've become a new creation in God, how the image of God still resides within you, as well as how that supernaturally enables you to do great things for Him.

You will also learn how God will help you stand in faith, making the impossible things possible. You will learn how to stand strong in the Lord against the attacks of the enemy, being aware of his strategies and being able to destroy them, by possessing the discerning of the spirits. God will show you specific information about people so you'll be able to help the greater body of Christ even though you are not physically present with those people. He will give you the ability to see, understand, and change the future of many people. These powerful experiences are awaiting you as you spend time in His presence.

I focus on a very important key throughout this book: praying in the spirit. Praying in the spirit will help you fulfill your destiny. Joseph fulfilled the dreams God gave him because he learned to walk in the Spirit. In the same way, when God has already spoken about your future, you can walk into it by praying in the spirit. In other words, praying in the spirit can transport you into another realm in order to get whatever is necessary for your future. It helps you get from point A to point Z. The enemy is always after believers, trying to destroy the plan of God for their lives. But through this gift you will stay connected with the Father, who has spoken the destiny over you. He will help you go further by aiding you in overcoming all the situations you encounter. This is going to be a mystery to those around you and to the enemy, but you will prosper and grow stronger in God because those mysteries are made evident by praying in the spirit. The first step to exponential growth in Christ is learning to pray in tongues while reading and meditating on the Word of God.

I encourage you to hold these keys closely as you walk with God: praying in the spirit, walking in faith by the Word of God, and staying hidden under the shadow of His wings while covered in His glory. After learning about and applying these keys, your life will be transformed. Many of you will begin to operate in these gifts as you express your desire through prayer.

But before we go any further in this book, let us agree together in prayer:

Lord Jesus, I pray for everyone who reads this book. Let it kindle the fire of God within them and make them more passionate to be in Your presence. As they desire the heavenly things, which You have already reserved for them, let it all be released in them so they can walk into the power and gifts of the Holy Spirit. Let their spiritual eyes be open to see into the unseen world. Let them do the impossible and let them bring Heaven down and change places and nations for You. In the mighty and powerful name of Jesus! Amen!

Chapter 1

Man Is A Spirit Being

The Bible says that man is a spirit, who has a soul and lives in a body. Most people are not aware that they are spiritual beings. In fact, it is important for people to know about their spirits if they are to fulfill their God-given destiny.

Looking at the way God created man will reveal many important aspects about our spirit. In the beginning God created man in His own image: "And God said, Let us make man in our image, after our likeness: and let them have dominion over the fish of the sea, and over the fowl of the air, and over the cattle, and over all the earth, and over every creeping thing that creepeth upon the earth. So God created man in his own image, in the image of God created he him; male and female created he them" (Genesis 1:26-27). God was a Spirit when He created man. Jesus said in John 4:24, "God is a Spirit…"

The Bible further tells us in Genesis 2:7, "And the LORD God formed man of the dust of the ground, and breathed into his nostrils the breath of life; and man became a living soul." By this we can see that although we are spirit beings, we also possess a physical body. We have many limitations because of our body—we are limited to a specific place at a specific time. God, on the other hand, is omnipresent, meaning He is present everywhere at all times. He has no limits because He is a Spirit and not trapped with a physical body.

The first man, Adam, lived in the glory of God before the Fall. He walked and talked with Him. God gave him power and dominion over all that was created. He had such knowledge and wisdom that he was able to name all the animals of the world and remember all of their names. Adam didn't lack anything. He had all he needed when God created him.

But death entered the human race when he sinned against God. Paul writes, "Wherefore, as by one man sin entered into the world, and death by sin; and so death passed upon all men, for that all have sinned…" (Romans 5:12). Adam was cut off from the presence of God because of his sin. Thus the curse entered and he began to lack in every area of his life.

He lost the authority and dominion he once had. He began to fear and had to now work and sweat to earn his food.

But praise God for Jesus! God sent His Son to redeem us from the curse (John 3:16; Galatians 3:13-14). When Jesus died on the cross, He took our sin and curses upon Himself. Through His death on the cross man could now come back to God. We could be restored to all Adam had lost when he sinned.

How was the human race restored? Through Jesus we can now approach God with boldness (Hebrews 4:16), where before there had been fear and shame. God restored us as His sons and daughters (John 1:12), where before there had been alienation. Jesus gave back to us the authority Adam lost so we could trample on the enemy (Luke 10:19). This means that health, blessings, and prosperity were restored to us as well (Isaiah 53:3-5; 2 Corinthians 8:9). And finally, Jesus promised us eternal life (Romans 6:23); not only that we would live with Him forever, but that we would possess a new kind of life while still in our physical bodies.

But before we go further, it is important to know more about our spirit and how it can cooperate with the Spirit of God.

Chapter 2

What Does Your Spirit Look Like?

I have an interesting question for you. Do you know what your spirit looks like? Very often people do not know how to answer when I ask them this question. If your spirit came out and stood next to you, what would it look like? What shape would it take? Would it have a personality? I believe it would look exactly like you—kind of like having a twin brother or sister. This may surprise some of you. But let's look at this in more detail, examining what the Bible says about this.

Jesus took Peter, James, and John to the Mount of Transfiguration to pray (Luke 9:28-36). All of the sudden Jesus began to shine, Moses and Elijah suddenly appeared with Him, talking with Him about His death and what had to take place in Jerusalem in the coming days. The disciples were afraid when they saw this. Why? I believe it was because some of them had physical bodies and others did not.

Among Jesus, Moses, and Elijah, do you know who had a physical body and who did not? It can be certain that Moses did not have a physical body because he had already died (Deuteronomy 34:5-6). Elijah had a physical body since he was taken up to Heaven alive (2 Kings 2:11). Jesus was also present in His physical body (Mark 9:2-4). The three disciples were able to clearly identify each of them, including Moses, who didn't have a physical body because he was already dead. The reason they could identify Moses was because the appearance of his spirit was similar to the appearance of his physical body.

We can also see a lot about how our spirits look like us from the story of the rich man and Lazarus:

> There was a certain rich man, which was clothed in purple and fine linen, and fared sumptuously every day: And there was a certain beggar named Lazarus, which was laid at his gate, full of sores, And desiring to be fed with the crumbs which fell from the rich man's table: more-

over the dogs came and licked his sores. And it came to pass, that the beggar died, and was carried by the angels into Abraham's bosom: the rich man also died, and was buried; And in hell he lift up his eyes, being in torments, and seeth Abraham afar off, and Lazarus in his bosom. And he cried and said, Father Abraham, have mercy on me, and send Lazarus, that he may dip the tip of his finger in water, and cool my tongue; for I am tormented in this flame. But Abraham said, Son, remember that thou in thy lifetime receivedst thy good things, and likewise Lazarus evil things: but now he is comforted, and thou art tormented. And beside all this, between us and you there is a great gulf fixed: so that they which would pass from hence to you cannot; neither can they pass to us, that *would come* from thence. Then he said, I pray thee therefore, father, that thou wouldest send him to my father's house: For I have five brethren; that he may testify unto them, lest they also come into this place of torment. Abraham saith unto him, They have Moses and the prophets; let them hear them. And he said, Nay, father Abraham: but if one went unto them from the dead, they will repent. And he said unto him, If they hear not Moses and the prophets, neither will they be persuaded, though one rose from the dead. — Luke 16:19-31

In this story both the rich man and Lazarus die. The rich man ended up in hell while the angels took Lazarus to the bosom of Abraham. Since both of them were dead they did not have physical bodies; they were spirits. They recognized each other though they were only spirits. The reason they could identify each other was the fact that the appearance of their spirits matched the appearance of their physical bodies. Both still possessed feelings and emotions. Both saw with their eyes and used physical speech (which they pronounced with their tongues) to communicate. They also heard what was being spoken because they both had ears.

Our spirits are eternal. Though our physical bodies will die and decay, we will live eternally—both believers and unbelievers. When we are washed by the blood of Jesus and have accepted Him as Lord and Savior of our lives, then we will eternally live with Him in Heaven. If a person has not done this, then when they die they will live eternally in hell. The truth is that everyone will live eternally—what we choose in this life reveals where we will live.

Jesus said, "And I say unto you my friends, Be not afraid of them that kill the body, and after that have no more that they can do. But I will forewarn you whom ye shall fear: Fear him, which after he hath killed hath power to cast into hell; yea, I say unto you, Fear him" (Luke 12:4-5). God is the one who judges and alone has authority to cast into hell (2 Corinthians 5:10).

It is clear from the above passages that, without a doubt, our spirits look just like our physical appearances.

Chapter 3

Taking Care Of Your Inner Man

The spirit of man is referred to as the inner man: "the inward man is renewed day by day" (2 Corinthians 4:16). When God speaks, He speaks to our spirit and not to our mind or our physical body. Job says, "But there is a spirit in man: and the inspiration of the Almighty giveth them understanding" (32:8). Therefore, we must take care of our spirits because that is where the Lord speaks to us and leads us.

Yet so often we don't take care of our inner man and end up in committing very costly mistakes. The state of our inner man determines how we live our lives as Christians. God performed extraordinary miracles through the life and ministry of Smith Wigglesworth—many dead people were brought to life through him. He once said, "My inner man is a thousand times bigger than my outward man." God powerfully used him because his inner man was strong in the Lord.

The Lord can see the inward parts of our spirit because our spirit is like a candle before Him—it is an open book before the Lord: "The spirit of man is the candle of the LORD, searching all the inward parts of the belly" (Proverbs 20:27). There is nothing that can be hidden in our spirits before God. This means that our spirit knows who we really are more than our natural mind knows. Getting connected with the Spirit of God makes a tremendous difference. The Spirit of God knows everything about our mind, our spirit, and our physical body.

Paul writes in 2 Corinthians 4:16, "But though our outward man perish, yet the inward man is renewed day by day." He is not only talking about a person's physical body getting old; but he is specifically talking about the believers who daily crucify their flesh (carnality). When they feed themselves with the Word of God and through the Spirit of God, these people can be renewed and grow stronger in their spirits.

When we listen to and obey the voice of God, He will be pleased. King David was described as a man after God's own heart because everything he did was bathed in prayer and a desire to be obedient to His will. The more we are obedient to His Spirit, the more we will mature and grow. The Spirit of God, who resides within us, is the Spirit of adoption, not the spirit that brings fear: "For as many as are led by the Spirit of God, they are the sons of God. For ye have not received the spirit of bondage again to fear; but ye have received the Spirit of adoption, whereby we cry, Abba, Father. The Spirit itself beareth witness with our spirit, that we are the children of God" (Romans 8:14-16).

When Paul saw some of the Corinthians wavering in their faith, he admonished them to grow in their spirits and become mature Christians (1 Corinthians 3:1-3). The situation today is very similar to what Paul saw in Corinth. I have seen a lot of people who have been born-again Christians for many years and are still "babies" in their spirits. They have been believers for ten or twenty years, and yet their spirits are still very weak and immature. A weak inner man cannot take on sin and overcome it. When people neglect to take care of their spirits, then the enemy attacks them in various ways because of their weakness. It is important for our inner man to be strong in order to lead a victorious Christian life.

When we receive Jesus into our hearts we become one spirit with Him (1 Corinthians 6:17). It is possible to be one with God since God is a Spirit and we are spirit beings. We were created in the image of God and bore that image perfectly until sin entered the world, then that image was lost. Now we are able to get back the same image of God as what was previously lost through adoption into Christ.

Second Corinthians 3:17-18 says, "Now the Lord is that Spirit: and where the Spirit of the Lord is, there is liberty. But we all, with open face beholding as in a glass the glory of the Lord, are changed into the same image from glory to glory, even as by the Spirit of the Lord." The Holy Spirit helps us grow from one degree of glory to the next. The Word of God, being led by the Spirit of God, walking by faith, and being obedient to Christ helps us grow stronger in the restored image of God. We can look like God on the inside once again.

Let me give you an example to help illustrate this. Suppose I take two drinking glasses that are full of water. Let's name the first one Glass A, and the second one Glass B. Glass A symbolizes God's Spirit while Glass B symbolizes man's spirit. Now suppose I took a drop of water from Glass A and put it into Glass B. Would you be able to recognize the drop of water in Glass B from the first glass? It's absolutely impossible since the drop has mixed with the water in Glass B. It has become one with the rest of the water.

Likewise, when we become one with Him, we are the majority; everything else in the world is the minority. We can see that we are one with God when we are born again. John confirms this when he writes: "Ye are of God, little children, and have overcome them: because greater is he that is in you, than he that is in the world" (1 John 4:4). Since God, who is greater than everything in all of creation, now resides within us, that causes us to look like Him in our spirit.

CHAPTER 4

Taking Away The Veil

Paul wrote about the veil that resided over the mind of unbelievers and how only in Christ that veil taken away. It blinds the mind and the heart, preventing people from understanding God's Word. Paul writes, "But their minds were blinded: for until this day remaineth the same vail untaken away in the reading of the old testament; which vail is done away in Christ. But even unto this day, when Moses is read, the vail is upon their heart. Nevertheless when it shall turn to the Lord, the vail shall be taken away. Now the Lord is that Spirit: and where the Spirit of the Lord is, there is liberty" (2 Corinthians 3:14-17).

The veil that blinds the heart and darkens the mind will only be taken away when someone turns to the Lord. The very next sentence says that the Lord is Spirit and there is liberty wherever the Spirit of the Lord is. There is a truth hidden in this passage that would do us well to understand. When we turn to the Lord and are filled with His Spirit, the veil on our hearts is taken away and we begin to understand the things of God in a uniquely new way. We begin to see what God wants us to see, and our inner man will understand the truths of the Word of God, which before were hidden from us.

A veiled mind is nothing more than the carnal mind Paul also wrote about elsewhere: "For to be carnally minded is death; but to be spiritually minded is life and peace. Because the carnal mind is enmity against God: for it is not subject to the law of God, neither indeed can be" (Romans 8:6-7). Then again, "But the natural man receiveth not the things of the Spirit of God: for they are foolishness unto him: neither can he know them, because they are spiritually discerned" (1 Corinthians 2:14).

A carnal mind impairs spiritual vision, keeping us from seeing how God wants us to see. The story about the Berlin Wall serves as an excellent example here, demonstrating how a veiled mind hinders a person from seeing the things of God. During the Cold War, West Germans could not see East Germans because the Berlin Wall separated them. It was quite high with no possible way for humans to look over to the other side by standing on the ground. The only way the West Germans could attempt to see East Germans was by standing on the roofs of tall buildings. They also had a second option, which was considered unthinkable at the time. That was to demolish the wall to meet their dear ones on the eastern side. Finally, when the Berlin Wall was demolished after the end of the Cold War, the West Germans and East Germans could see each other face to face. Likewise, people with veiled minds have a wall of separation between them and God, which does not allow them to see what the Lord wants them to see. Unless the Lord demolishes that wall, then they cannot see the things of God.

I believe that carnality is a huge problem in the church. When our five physical senses are not submitted to the Holy Spirit, our minds become carnal. This is why Christians must be careful about what they see, hear, touch, smell, and taste. And all of this begins in the mind—we need to be careful about what we think about.

As we allow carnality to stay in our minds, at the same time it also becomes a stronghold. For example, seeing and hearing bad things can negatively affect our minds. It can also be affected and controlled by the circumstances surrounding us. We naturally intend to follow what we see, hear, and feel—we are thoroughly dependent on our physical senses. This is why we often fail to see the mighty things of God. All the strongholds (fear, doubt, anger, jealousy, etc.) that are built up in our minds will bring limitations. Not only limitations, but these strongholds will also control our whole system of thinking and acting.

Only when our minds are unveiled can we begin to see how much God has blessed us. It is only then that we can begin to look on our life and circumstances through the eyes of Christ. Consider the burning wick of a lantern for a moment. Many years ago people used lanterns to light their rooms. They gave off light by lighting the wick, which was soaked in oil or kerosene. If the light is kept burning all the time, it would produce a lot of smoke, darkening the glass around the wick. That is why it was important to trim the wick and not leave it burning at all times.

Your spirit is much like the burning wick while the glass is much like your mind. When the glass is not clean and the soot from the smoke is clouding it, then the light cannot pass through it in the way it was created to. Though the wick is burning brightly and is still giving light, this light cannot be seen outside. Our minds get contaminated with different thoughts and circumstances, becoming filled with disturbances and confusions. It is during these times we don't feel the presence or the peace of God. However, we should know that our spirit is still burning inside of us; and all the gifts, peace, and blessings are inside as well. But many times because our minds are darkened we don't experience these good things.

Chapter 5

Losing Your Identity Through Fear

We have been learning about the spirit of a man. Man is a spirit being and we have learned how God created him in His own image. After this, however, man sinned against God and somehow lost that image in its fullness—it was marred. Fear entered into him because it is one of the products of sin. The first words out of Adam's mouth when he sinned were, "I was afraid" (Genesis 3:10). Man couldn't directly approach God with sin and fear; something had to take place. Adam walked in God's glory without any sense of fear, not lacking any good thing, before he fell into sin. He enjoyed God's love and longed for His friendship. He had more than what he needed when he was in God's glory. Even the Bible says that the rivers which were in the Garden brought forth all the precious stones and gold (Genesis 2:11-12).

But fear entered with the presence of sin; and fear brings torment. Solomon wrote, "The fear of man bringeth a snare…" (Proverbs 29:25). Fear destroys the identity of God in man. Job said after being attacked by the enemy under the permission of God, "For the thing which I greatly feared has come upon me, and that which I was afraid of is come unto me" (3:25). Fear opens a door to the enemy if it is not dealt with. That which you are afraid of can come upon you. Fear is not from God.

Even though Elijah was a mighty prophet of God, used to call down fire on His enemies, he was still crippled by fear and fled for his life, wanting to die under a tree.

> And Ahab told Jezebel all that Elijah had done, and withal how he had slain all the prophets with the sword. Then Jezebel sent a messenger unto Elijah, saying, So let the gods do to me, and more also, if I make not thy life as the life of one of them by to morrow about this time. And when he saw that, he arose, and went for his life, and came to Beersheba, which belongeth to Judah, and left his servant there. — 1 Kings 19:1-3

Elijah fled away from Jezebel in fear when she said that she wanted to kill him. He acted very differently when fear was present than how he normally acted in its absence. He forgot how he stood with boldness and faith in the prophetic anointing and brought the fire down from Heaven. It was out of character for him to run and hide for his life. Then the angel of God brought food for him and he went in the strength of God for forty days. God met him and asked what he was doing sitting under the tree. Elijah tried to explain how the people were killing prophets and he alone has survived. God was trying to tell him that he would have done more mighty acts, but because of fear he missed out on what God had planned for him. God wanted Elijah to anoint Nimshi and another prophet, Elisha, to take over his office.

We often lose many blessings and act very differently in various situations because of fear. Sometimes we don't hold on to the truth and we end up compromising. This happens even though we need to be bold and courageous, filled with faith. Paul reminded Timothy, "For God hath not given us the spirit of fear; but of power, and of love, and of a sound mind" (2 Timothy 1:7). And the Proverbs also remind us, "For as he thinketh in his heart, so is he" (23:7).

Fear has the potential to torment every human. Until you are delivered from that particular fear, it will continue to torment you. Numbers 13 tells the story of the Israelites and how they lost their identity because of fear. They forgot who they were and all that God promised them.

God told Moses to choose twelve leaders, one from each tribe. Then He instructed them to search the land of Canaan, which flows with milk and honey. When the twelve leaders went into the land, they saw the land was prosperous and the fruit of it was very good. It was filled with huge pomegranates and grapes. The cluster of grapes was so huge that two men had to carry a single cluster back to the camp! The leaders returned and began to report to Moses all that they saw. Everything God had promised them was right—the land was prosperous and flowing with milk and honey.

However, they also reported what they were afraid of: the people who lived there were very strong. They were like giants and the Israelites were like grasshoppers in their sight. They began to compare themselves with that nation, thinking they were nobodies and forgetting everything God had promised them about their future. They began to talk more about their enemies and less about who their God was. Though God chose them and gave them a promise that He would give them the land, fear entered in and they began to forget who they were and the promises of God. They began to act differently. They saw themselves as grasshoppers in their own sight. They were essentially losing their identity in God. The leaders' fear brought fear into the entire camp of Israel. The whole camp wept, cried, and complained against God and Moses, which made God upset.

But there were two people, however, Joshua and Caleb, who knew who they were and knew who their God was. They remembered the promises of God even in the midst of trying circumstances. They said they were more than able to take the land and be victorious over the people living there. Whereas fear was destroying the others' identity and the leaders were acting cowardly instead of bold, Joshua and Caleb rose up to declare that since God has promised it, He would do it and fight for them. Remember that "as [a man] thinketh in his heart, so is he" (Proverbs 23:7). The ten leaders began to think that they were very insignificant, forgetting about their Creator, the Powerful God who promised them that He would give them that prosperous land. But Caleb and Joshua were different. They weren't bound by fear.

Everything we see around us has been created by His words. Even when He came down to meet with Moses on Mt.

Sinai, the Bible says that the mountain shook and smoked because of His presence. He is so powerful and loves us and lives in us! When our senses get messed up and we begin to focus on other things more than God, things are going to fail every time. When my mind is attacked by fear, confusion, and doubt, I am going down hill fast. In that place God asks us to focus on Him and all He has done for us.

I want to share with you some of my own story of how God lifted me up from all kinds of problems. A few years ago our family was going through many challenges. Almost every one of us was getting sick, there were financial burdens, and many other things seemed to be going wrong. I constantly faced all of these problems through day and night prayer. I didn't feel God and didn't see any of my prayers getting answered either. The devil began putting doubt in my mind. I began thinking God was upset with me or I had some sin in my life that I wasn't aware of. I began to constantly search my heart and pray, but I didn't find anything wrong with me. All the while the circumstances were becoming worse and worse. I was physically worn out and mentally tormented. So one day I decided that I just had to talk with God—I had to get some results.

I was in the living room by myself at night, very disappointed and without any physical strength. I stood against the wall lifting my arms up to God. And I began to pray, "Lord, You know how I feel today. I don't feel good. You know that. I don't feel Your presence. I don't care how I am feeling. I don't care how many demons are standing next to me. But one thing I know is that Your presence is with me. I don't see You and I don't feel You, but You are looking at me. I know Your presence is with me because You promised that Your presence would go with me. Thank You for being with me today." Then I began to depend on one Scripture—that He is with me. I continued to praise Him, "Thank You, God, for being with me. Thank You for Your sweet presence. You are keeping Your promises to me. Because of Your promise, You are with me tonight." I continued to repeat these same words. And after about an hour of doing this I began to feel peace coming into my heart. My hands and feet very slowly become warm. The heat increased as I kept praising and thanking God for His presence. Not only my hands and my feet, but also my whole body began to be so warm as if I was standing in a hot fire. I was so excited and encouraged by this! I knew for sure He was in my room with me!

Suddenly God opened my eyes. I saw the consuming fire of God going all around me. I said, "Wow! Wow! What power from God!" And then thought, "If anyone throws dead bodies in this place, they will be raised up!" It is hard to describe the intense amount of power going on around me. I was suddenly taken out of my house while this was going on and saw it from the outside. I saw many demons all around. Then I saw an angel of God come down and immediately chased all the demons away. The next thing I knew was that I was back in my living room—feeling like I was thrown back from space. I was so excited, yet wondered what happened to me. God spoke to me very clearly, "My son, stop looking at those demons. Stop looking at your problems. Focus on Me." That was the key that helped us come out of many problems we had been experiencing. Praise God for His love and His presence!

On a particular night many years ago I was tired. I slept in my room for a few hours and woke up at two in the morning. I remembered I had already slept a lot, so I needed to pray. During those days I would go outside to walk and pray so I wouldn't fall asleep. Since my house was in the countryside without any other houses nearby, this proved to be very helpful. I went out into the dark, still half asleep and half awake. I really didn't know where I was walking. But as I continued to walk in the dark, I heard footsteps behind me. When I turned back to see who was there, there was nobody. Fear immediately gripped me. I walked a little further and was able to hear the sound of the footsteps louder and closer than before. At that point I was fully awake because I was so scared! I thought that I should just scream and run back home. The truth is that when you are attacked by fear, you don't think much about God in the moment. The only thing you think about is the fear that is present.

There was a little thought that crept into my mind in the midst of the fear: God was with me. I had to decide in that moment whether I should scream and run back home or hold onto this word that God was with me. I forced myself to think about God, and began speaking that God was with me. I said, "Thank You, Jesus, You are with me." Though there was such a struggle in my heart as the fear tried to consume me, I tried to say that God was with me over and over again. In the midst of the struggle I began to feel a little bit of peace coming into my heart. So I repeatedly said, "Thank You, Jesus, for being with me and thank You for Your presence," as I lifted my hands to Heaven. All of my attention went to the sky. I suddenly heard a beautiful sound which I never heard in my life. It sounded like many small bells were ringing together, but it was like they were all singing. Then the clouds in the sky become colorful and, moreover, I saw Heaven open up. A man came down and stood before me. He was dressed like a medieval warrior—wearing a metal skirt, armor, and holding a big sword. I heard the metal pieces around his waist banging against each other as he touched the ground. As he stood before me, I immediately heard God's voice say, "My son, don't be afraid. I have sent My angel. His name is Michael. He will protect you." It was as if His voice carried thousands of volts of electricity and flowed through my body. I received strength and boldness from His voice. When it was all over, I looked at my watch. It was five o'clock in the morning! The experience changed my life.

Now, whenever I need help from God, God sends His angels to protect me and help me to minister to those around me (Psalm 91; Psalm 37).

CHAPTER 6

Controlled By The Wrong Spirit

When our minds are sensitive and weak, the wrong spirit can often then control them. When tuning the radio to find a different station, there is often a point where two stations overlap and you can hear both of them at the same time. Sometimes the signal for a particular station is really good while at others times it is really weak. The mind can also act in a very similar way as this—it can be controlled and pick up signals from the wrong spirit.

Have you ever been in a store where a song is being played, and as you hear it you don't intend to sing along with it, but as you're driving away you find yourself singing or humming that same tune you just heard? This can happen when you pick up on the wrong spirits as well. When you are spending time with the wrong person, maybe that person is controlled by a demon or is just talking bad, you seem to notice heaviness or a headache at the end of the day. And you wonder why that is happening to you. Picking up on the wrong spirit may be one of the reasons.

Some people are in situations where they have to work with difficult people, people swearing and continually using profanity. You may find yourself beginning to utter those same words every now and then, or they simply slip out of your mouth on occasion. That is the force of the spirit the other person is carrying. Or maybe you have experienced a person who is angry or short tempered; in the end you will behave like that person if you choose to continually walk with them.

What we often call people's personalities are just different spirits controlling them. Some of the most common are anger, lust, and jealousy; while some of the worse things are witchcraft, black magic, and voodoo. There are all kinds of people living in the world controlled by the wrong spirit. Many times without our knowledge we interact with them. Many of the people under the influence of these spirits will try to control our lives; and sometimes if we don't do what they want, then they will try to curse us or control us through spirits they are carrying. Jesus prayed that though we are in the world, we would not be affected by this world (John 17:15-19).

We have the Spirit of God living in us, which makes all the difference. This is why John declares, "For whatsoever is born of God overcometh the world: and this is the victory that overcometh the world, even our faith" (1 John 5:4). This means that if we are washed by the blood of Jesus and filled with the Holy Spirit, then when we are put into this kind of situation, we will feel uncomfortable or uneasy inside. We won't feel peace in that situation. We may feel like we are choked—just like a fish out of water—which is one of the first steps of the discerning of spirits. But it is important to remember that God has given us authority over the situation or circumstances surrounding us. When we are sensitive to the Holy Spirit, we can change the circumstances by the Word and the Spirit of God. The first thing we have to try to do is not get into these situations. But if we are forced to, then with God's help we can change the circumstances by the power of the Spirit.

First Samuel 16:22-23 says, "And Saul sent to Jesse, saying, Let David, I pray thee, stand before me; for he hath found favor in my sight. And it came to pass, when the evil spirit from God was upon Saul, that David took an harp, and played with his hand: so Saul was refreshed, and was well, and the evil spirit departed from him."

King Saul was disobedient to the Lord, which opened him up for the demon to attack him. However, every time David played the harp the demon would leave and Saul would become peaceful. Worship brought the presence of God and drove out the demonic realm. We need to stay in the glory of God in order to keep the devil and the oppression out of our way. If we don't stay under His glory and covered by His Word, and if we don't influence others by the presence that we carry, they will try to influence us back. But it is important to remember that you "are of God, little children, and have overcome them: because greater is he that is in you, than he that is in the world" (1 John 4:4).

Some time ago I was traveling with a few people to minister. When we went to one of the larger meetings, another young man also joined us. Whenever we were talking about different aspects of the Kingdom of God, about the ministry, and what happens during meetings, this man would join the conversation. When he was there, there was absolutely no agreement or unity. I began to feel very uncomfortable every time he would talk. He also stayed with us in one of the larger rooms we were all staying in. He was in the corner sleeping by himself while everyone else was also asleep. As I was praying, I began to feel very heavy and struggled to pray. Suddenly my spiritual eyes were opened and I saw the demon popping out of this man's head and coming towards me to attack. After seeing this a few times, the Holy Spirit empowered me with the anointing to break that demonic power. The next day I talked with this man and prayed for his deliverance. God set him free.

Another time a friend of mine asked me to pray for his family because they were going through a lot of problems. There were arguments, strife, sickness, and no peace in their home. There were a few families who lived together in one big house. The first day I was there I was sitting on the couch praying. I saw the devil come like a goat and try to attack them. I kicked it on the head and felt the horn under my feet for two days afterwards. God showed me a lady who was in that house that was controlled by the devil, being used by him to control everyone else in the house. Many times these kinds of people will be found in churches, not to mention other places too.

Fear is a contaminator of faith. Not only will it keep us away from God, it will also make us feel far away from Him. One of its big effects can be a misunderstanding between our

Heavenly Father and us. We begin to doubt His presence and His love for us, which grieves the Holy Spirit. Whichever is dominant, either our spirit or our mind, will lead the way for the other to follow. For example, if we are led by the Spirit of God and filled with the Word of God, our spirit man will be more active and obedient to His promptings. He will be able to receive more from God. However, if our natural mind is contaminated with fear and doubt, it will take us away from God's ways. This is why Paul reminds us, "For to be carnally minded is death; but to be spiritually minded is life and peace" (Romans 8:6).

When we think about how we were created, it looks like we have two different personalities. That is to say that we are spiritually filled and led by the Spirit of God, and then there are the times we are carnally minded. One will get information from God and the other will try to get information from other sources. The Bible interestingly describes this: "For the word of God is quick, and powerful, and sharper than any twoedged sword, piercing even to the dividing asunder of soul and spirit, and of the joints and marrow, and is the discerner of the thoughts and intents of the heart" (Hebrews 4:12). Reading and meditating on God's Word will bring such an affect upon us—to separate the mind from the spirit.

In other words, it creates two different channels whereby we can pick up signals. One is for discerning of the thoughts, which will come from our mind; the other channel is to discern the intention of the heart, which will be from our spirit man. The Word of God has power to distinguish between the two!

However, when we stand on God's Word and believe what it says, which can sometimes be contrary against our circumstances or even nature itself, we will see great and mighty things. For example, when Moses and the Israelites came to the Red Sea, it was impossible for them to walk through to the other side. Through the natural limitations it was impossible, but God was able to do it against nature by dividing the sea so they could walk through on dry ground. Another time when Jesus was on the mountain praying (John 6:19), He sensed that His disciples, who were in the boat in the middle of the night, were in trouble because of the wind. Jesus came early in the morning to help them. The disciples were scared because they didn't naturally know how Jesus could walk on the water, which was again against the laws of nature. Humans cannot naturally do this because of the law of gravity. All people have physical and mental limitations, but Jesus was able to walk on the water, speaking comfort to them, and thus save them.

Then we also see in Mark 5:35-43 Jesus going to Jairus' house to heal his daughter. But on the way, one of his servant's came and told him that his daughter was dead. Before Jairus could say anything, Jesus said to him, "Be not afraid, only believe." Later on we see Jesus raising his daughter from the dead. Again, it is impossible for this to happen under natural laws. But the Bible says that "all things are possible to him that believeth" (Mark 9:23).

I hope you now understand how many limitations we have in our life, but praise God that Jesus is the same yesterday, today and forever! The same God who parted the Red Sea is still alive today. The one who raised the dead, who healed the blind, who restores everything to perfect order, is the one still with us today!

Chapter 7

Breaking Strongholds From Your Mind

Paul writes to the Corinthians about how to break strongholds off their minds:

> For though we walk in the flesh, we do not war after the flesh: (For the weapons of our warfare are not carnal, but mighty through God to the pulling down of strong holds;) Casting down imaginations, and every high thing that exalteth itself against the knowledge of God, and bringing into captivity every thought to the obedience of Christ.
> — 2 Corinthians 10:3-5

The weapons God gives us are strong and mighty, and through them we can pull down the strongholds of the devil.

The devil can use our weaknesses to build a stronghold in our minds. It can be worries, fear, wrong thoughts, or differing imaginations. It can be a spirit of lust or a spirit of anger, which are built up in our mind through demonic powers. These strongholds work against us and God's plans for our lives, thus causing harm. Not only do they affect us, but through them others can be affected as well, even your own family. These thoughts and strongholds don't easily submit to us, but instead they war against us. But praise God that if we are a believer, washed by the blood of Jesus, then He who lives in us can give us strength and spiritual weapons through the Holy Spirit and the Word of God. We can pull down the strongholds of the devil.

People who commit adultery or physical abuse do so because of all the spirits which are actively working in their lives. These spirits enter because those people opened the door by disobeying God and sinning. Allowing these spirits access causes people to repeatedly fall into the same sin. Most everyone knows what is right and what is wrong. However, when it comes to doing the right things and forsaking the wrong things, they are not able to do it in their own power. Instead they fall into the same weaknesses and sin because of the force of the stronghold that is controlling them.

Chapter 8

The Discerning Of Spirits

Part of breaking strongholds off our mind is through being able to discern the presence of spirits around us. We are engaged in a war that can't be seen with the physical eyes or fought with natural weapons. Paul admonished the Ephesians:

> Finally, my brethren, be strong in the Lord, and in the power of his might. Put on the whole armor of God, that ye may be able to stand against the wiles of the devil. For we wrestle not against flesh and blood, but against principalities, against powers, against the rulers of the darkness of this world, against spiritual wickedness in high places.
> — Ephesians 6:10-12

He was trying to prepare the believers to be strong in the power of God by putting on the armor of God.

There are different categories of demonic spirits that strategically operate in the world today. Principalities are the highest form of demonic forces, next to Satan. They are chief rulers and beings of the first rank and order in their own kingdom. They directly receive their orders from Satan.

The next are powers, which we see as authorities, derived from and constituted by above. They use their demonic power for false miracles and they impact people by controlling them. They also bring their influence upon leaders of the world, thereby controlling them and exerting force in the nations.

The third category of demonic spirits Paul talks about is the rulers of the darkness of this world. They are the spiritual beings of wickedness, the emperor of the darkness of this state of things. They are territorial demons that take control over entire towns and even cities.

And then there are what Paul calls spiritual wickedness, which are the spiritual beings of wickedness. They are highly refined and sublimed evil, disguised falsehood in the cloak of truth. They include false gods and false religions. All of the evil wickedness—drugs, murder, prostitution, and any other bad thing you can think of—is influenced and controlled by this category of demons.

People behave very differently when they are blinded by demons. They can be aggressive, even going to the extent of killing people. Territorial demons can influence whole towns with one major sin. Some towns are full of witchcraft, voodoo, black magic, etc. These things can be seen in one part of a town or the entire town may be practicing them. Other towns may see different areas filled with prostitution or adultery, mixed with drugs.

When I was in Hamburg, Germany, preparing for my evening meeting, I was praying in the spirit and meditating on God's Word. In the middle of my prayer I felt heavy and tired. I was forcing myself to continue to pray; and as I did, the Holy Spirit opened my eyes to see in the realm of the spirit around me. There were demons standing all around me. They were trying to come closer to me in order to attack me. I could tell they were very upset and they didn't like me being in their city. But the good news is that they couldn't come any closer to touch me because of the power of the Spirit! I recognized them by the Holy Spirit—or what Paul calls the "discerning of spirits" (1 Corinthians 12:10). I knew there was a spirit of alcohol, a spirit of drugs, a spirit of prostitution, and a spirit of infirmities. Several of them were there trying to attack me. But as I continued to pray in tongues, the Holy Spirit fell upon me and build me up in my faith.

And then I saw another scene. There was another demon coming down from the ceiling, much more ugly and stronger than the others. I knew he too was coming to attack me. He came towards me very quickly. The Holy Spirit brought such an anointing upon me as Jesus' name automatically came from my mouth. The power of God was released, blasting the ugliest demon away. As soon as it happened, all the other demons disappeared along with it.

Wondering what all this was about, that same evening when I went to minister, the Holy Spirit was already profoundly present. While I was preaching, conviction came heavily upon the people as I gave an altar call. Many people came to the front, crying and giving their lives to Jesus. To my surprise, those people who came to the front were prostitutes, drug addicts, and alcoholics. Not only that, but also many people that came with sicknesses and infirmities were healed. Praise God for these wonderful gifts! God has given us this power to deliver people from darkness and bring them into the light.

My wife Tammy and I, along with some friends, were traveling in the southern part of Germany, which borders Switzerland. As we were entering the town that we were to minister in that evening, God supernaturally showed me that witches were sacrificing babies; He also revealed to me that there was a lot of witchcraft present as well. When the meeting started that evening, Tammy picked out a woman from the crowd and prayed for her. Through the word of knowledge and prophetic words, God began to reveal to Tammy about this woman's past—how she was sexually abused, but also about how God protected her from death. We happened to meet with this woman afterwards and she began to cry as she told us her story.

She said that the town she is from is very much known for witches. The witches sacrifice young children frequently. Her own father, who was a witch, along with other witches, sexually abused her during those satanic rituals. They dragged her to the place where they were going to sacrifice her, but somehow God's hand came upon her and she was protected. She was so wounded and hurt from those experiences, desperately needing to be healed and delivered. Praise God that He touched her in our meetings!

During the time of Daniel we see that the prince of Persia, one of the rulers of the air, came to fight against the angel of God (Daniel 10). Daniel was influencing the whole kingdom of Babylon by the power of God, with his God-given wisdom. For Daniel to operate in this dimension took total dedication to God. Daniel risked his life to not eat or drink the wrong things so he would keep himself holy before God (Daniel 1). He didn't compromise with the wrong religion; even his friends stood for truth. Demons couldn't do anything to him because of his dedication to God and the faith he had in Him. So the bigger territorial demon tried to come against the angel of God and hinder the blessing Daniel was praying for. We can influence cities, towns, and even kingdoms as we grow spiritually strong.

Even though Satan deceived and stole the authority Adam possessed in the beginning, the blood of Jesus bought it back for us. We are the children of God and have all authority and power that has been given to us by Jesus. We are restored to dominion and authority once again. Not only that, but when Jesus died on the cross of Calvary, according to Colossians 2, He broke the demonic power, stripping him, and making an open show of him. We have all the blessings and dominion now through Christ.

Satan asked Jesus that if He would bow down and worship him, then he would give Jesus all the kingdoms of the world. Instead of worshipping him, Jesus rebuked him and told him that all the worship would go to God. Later on Jesus stripped everything from Satan through the cross and gave us, the body of Christ, the keys of the Kingdom. Those who stand in this truth, being complete in Jesus, can take city after city and nation after nation with the victory of God.

When I minister in evangelistic crusades in a town, my fellow intercessors and I pray (sometimes with fasting) for that particular town before we arrive. Many times God has shown us the demons that are operating in that town. We take authority over those demons, casting them out of the town along with breaking their strongholds, and then asking God to release His blessings on the town. This often causes great breakthrough at our meetings because we have already paved the way through prayer beforehand.

We must take His Word into our spirit because it will never fail us—it is strong and powerful. It always accomplishes what it says. The Word of God is an offensive weapon in the armor God has given us to withstand the attacks of the enemy (Ephesians 6:11-18).

It is vital that we are covered by the blood of Jesus and standing in righteousness, without any sense of shame or guilt, coming to God with boldness. Being bold against the demonic forces, knowing that Jesus is our Lord, wearing all the armor of God, and being full of the Holy Spirit and His Word, we are enabled to overcome all situations the demonic powers create.

If a preacher is truly called to speak or teach, they will have certain kinds of opposition from the enemy before they ever begin their ministry. If that same preacher begins to have a bigger dream or vision, he will have even more opposition by much more powerful demons. And any man or woman of God who tries to go deeper than this, just like Daniel and Paul were able to do, then they will see greater opposition. The higher we go with God, the more opposition we're going to face throughout our life.

As God begins to use people more and more, then the enemy tries to tempt most of them with pride, women, and money. If we are not careful, then there is a danger to falling into one of these traps. Many cannot withstand the temptation, fall into sin, and their marriage ends in divorce. So when God begins to bless you and lift you up, you need to keep yourself humble and always surrounded by men of God who pray for you and who stand in agreement with you. One of the patterns of Jesus is to stand together as the body of Christ. If two are three are gathered in His name, He promised He would be with us (Matthew 18:20). And we need to remember that Jesus sent His disciples out two by two—there is power in numbers. But we should also know that God will always give His angels to protect us. So be wise and led by the Spirit of God.

The territorial spirits don't like it when the person who is fully anointed by God goes to different nations. They try to stop what these men and women of God bring to their realm. If that anointed person enters the realm they have been dominating, then they know he can destroy the demonic realm by the power of the Holy Spirit.

God has given me different supernatural experiences as I have traveled to different parts of the world. There have been different territorial and regional demons that have come to attack me, but Jesus supernaturally came and protected me. He has always sent His angels to guard me and protect me. He has taken me to many dangerous places. I have stayed with witch doctors and those in the mafia without even knowing it. I have also travelled to interior places where all the bad things happen. But in every circumstance, God's hand was upon me to protect me.

When God begins to use us in different dimensions, He will begin to show us how the places are affected by the different types of demons present. When that demonic power is broken and people are saved and delivered, then God's Kingdom comes with power. God has taken me to places during prayer times where people practice witchcraft or are involved in drugs. With the power of God He has helped me to break strongholds in many different places through the power of prayer.

In September 2011 I felt such opposition in the spiritual realm as I was praying, fasting, and worshipping God. It was around three in the morning as God took me into the spiritual realm. He first showed me what was going to happen in the coming days of our ministry. He then took me to certain places in the world to pray for those specific places. I saw people who were demonized and tried to catch me as I was traveling through their towns. But they couldn't because I was under the control of the Holy Spirit. God carried me to a higher level through those experiences. Then, later on, the Holy Spirit showed me different places that were infected by sin and demons—the strongholds there had not been broken by anyone. The sins of the past were affecting the present generation. I knew the families of the present generation, but I didn't know anything that had happened in the past until God revealed it to me. I was enabled by the power of God to destroy the strongholds, so the people, who had been controlled by them, could be delivered. What oftentimes happens in the past can affect the present and even the future.

God tells us to forget the past because He is about to do a new thing in our life (Isaiah 43:18-19). Then God told Moses to tell the people of Israel: "Thou shalt not bow down thyself to them, nor serve them: for I the LORD thy God am a jealous God, visiting the iniquity of the fathers upon the children unto the third and fourth generation of them that hate me; And shewing mercy unto thousands of them that love me, and keep my commandments" (Exodus 20:5-6). The curses of one generation can transfer to the next, bringing the same old problems to the younger generation. The curses include all the bad and evil things—sin, sickness, poverty, demonic spirits, etc.

But they can be easily broken by confessing our sins, asking Jesus to cleanse us with His blood, and asking Him to break every curse that has come upon us from past generations. It is also good to ask Jesus to bless us and our generation with all the blessings of God (Galatians 3:13-14). Jesus became a curse for us so that we could receive the blessings of Abraham. We are able to receive good health, strength, prosperity, and peace through the blessings of God. This is so simple and yet so powerful if we believe what God's Word declares. We will receive all the blessings in Christ.

Sometimes people need a certain type of deliverance. Though some are saved and washed by the blood of Jesus, no doubt children of God, but because of the lack of knowledge of the Word of God and not knowing the truth, they can still be in bondage. They need the help of anointed people to pray for them. Through the authority and power of the Holy Spirit they can break the demonic bondage over their lives. If you are not walking in the freedom of the Holy Spirit, there is a possibility that the enemy is attacking you through unbelief and fear. So stand strong and believe the promise of God for you. You don't need to go through the same problem that the past generation went through. Be blessed and stay blessed.

Paul told Timothy about seducing spirits that would come in the last days: "Now the Spirit speaketh expressly, that in the latter times some shall depart from the faith, giving heed to seducing spirits, and doctrines of devils" (1 Timothy

4:1). We also know there is wickedness in high places as well (Ephesians 6:10-12). These seducing spirits and wickedness in high places can deceive people, causing them to fall into false teaching and false religions. We also see many wrong interpretations of the Bible by spirits as well. Do you remember when Satan came to tempt Jesus? He didn't come with flat out lies, but he came with the twisted Word of God.

When God taught me how to pray in the spirit, I also learned the importance of reading and meditating on the Word of God. In between my reading and mediation, I would sing and worship God. This took me into different directions in the spiritual realm. God began to bless me and bless others through what was happening. He will often give us something to bless others with.

For example, if God gives you the gift of healing and you don't want to pray for the sick, then what's the purpose in Him giving you the gift? Or, in the same way, if you have the gift of prophecy but don't want to prophesy than there is no use in you having the gift. Whatever the gift or talent that God gives to you, use it for the Kingdom of God. As you begin to speak in tongues, read the Bible, worship, walk in humility, love God, and walk in holiness, there will be things that will begin to change faster and God will begin to open your eyes to see what is unseen with the natural senses.

Discerning of spirits is a gift from God given to us through the Holy Spirit, revealing to us the type of spirit people have. Because we are living in really bad days, people will come with a smile, act like a good Christian, but many times their secret life is really bad. Sometimes they will carry wrong spirits. Some will operate with familiar spirits, communicate with the dead, or be involved in witchcraft, and other such things. That's why it is very important to have this particular gift of the Holy Spirit. It will help us discern the spirits that men and women are carrying. The Holy Spirit will help us in many uncomfortable places that may be contaminated by evil spirits, helping us discern what is taking place there. God will not only show us what is operating there, but He will give us the authority and power to destroy the demonic powers and bring the Kingdom of God.

The word of wisdom, word of knowledge, and the discerning of spirits all fall under the category of revelation gifts. These are written in 1 Corinthians 12. The revelation gifts mostly operate in prophets. Usually the prophet will operate in almost all of the gifts of the Spirit, but these will be their primary gifts. In the Old Testament, the prophet was called a seer; meaning they would see and hear more clearly than other believers. The secrets of God can be revealed through these gifts.

When the discerning of spirits is in operation, it can connect us to the word of knowledge, the word of wisdom, the gift of faith, and the working of miracles. We will not operate by ourselves in these gifts, but the Holy Spirit will enable us to operate in them. God may reveal to you specific information about a person or a place. He may show you about the demonic influence or demonic possession that is operating. And then God will suddenly fill you with faith and authority to break that demonic power which is holding that person or place captive. He may also give you deeper knowledge about people, about their physical condition or their past history. God will bring angels on the scene to protect the person who is operating in the gifts of the Spirit or bringing a message from God. Then the healing or miracle will take place. All of the gifts of the Spirit are beautifully designed for the whole benefit of the body of Christ, to be filled with the Holy Spirit in order to bring salvation, healing, and miracles into the lives of people. We literally bring the Kingdom of God down into our present realm.

When Jesus told His disciples to go to the other side of the lake, He fell asleep in the boat while they were crossing the lake (Luke 8:22-33). They all began to panic when a storm hit their boat. But Jesus already knew he was going on a special mission—He knew there was a demonized man on the other side that needed deliverance. The storm they faced was not normal; rather, it was a storm created by demons, because the demons in the man could sense Jesus was coming. When demons become aware of a man of God coming into town, they try to come against him, stop him, or create some kind of confusion or problem so he can't enter the town God is sending him into. The demons create a storm to try to stop Jesus from entering their town, but Jesus already possesses all authority over the wind and waves, over all of creation. He could calm the storm and deliver this man out of demon possession.

Now read the way Luke describes the story with fresh eyes and uplifted faith:

> Now it came to pass on a certain day, that he went into a ship with his disciples: and he said unto them, Let us go over unto the other side of the lake. And they launched forth. But as they sailed he fell asleep: and there came

down a storm of wind on the lake; and they were filled *with water*, and were in jeopardy. And they came to him, and awoke him, saying, Master, master, we perish. Then he arose, and rebuked the wind and the raging of the water: and they ceased, and there was a calm. And he said unto them, Where is your faith? And they being afraid wondered, saying one to another, What manner of man is this! for he commandeth even the winds and water, and they obey him. And they arrived at the country of the Gadarenes, which is over against Galilee. And when he went forth to land, there met him out of the city a certain man, which had devils long time, and ware no clothes, neither abode in *any* house, but in the tombs. When he saw Jesus, he cried out, and fell down before him, and with a loud voice said, What have I to do with thee, Jesus, *thou* Son of God most high? I beseech thee, torment me not. (For he had commanded the unclean spirit to come out of the man. For oftentimes it had caught him: and he was kept bound with chains and in fetters; and he brake the bands, and was driven of the devil into the wilderness.) And Jesus asked him, saying, What is thy name? And he said, Legion: because many devils were entered into him. And they besought him that he would not com-

mand them to go out into the deep. And there was there an herd of many swine feeding on the mountain: and they besought him that he would suffer them to enter into them. And he suffered them. Then went the devils out of the man, and entered into the swine: and the herd ran violently down a steep place into the lake, and were choked.
— Luke 8:22-33

Do you remember when King David was supposed to go to war? He didn't go, but instead was tempted by seeing Bathsheba and fell into sin. I want every man and woman of God to listen to me very carefully at this point. When you are going on a special mission for God, there is always going to be temptation, trouble, confusion, arguments, disunity, etc. All of this comes from demonic influences so you will not fulfill God's will. When God is about to perform a mighty miracle in your life, there will always be some kind of temptation before that point. If you are a man of God, you may get tempted to fall into the sin of adultery. Or if you are a woman, you will have a different type of temptation. You must keep yourself clean and holy if you are dealing with these kinds of things.

Even when David was young and heard the challenge from Goliath, he knew he could defeat him because he had already learned to defeat the bear and the lion as he was tending his father's sheep. He knew, by God's help, he could defeat the giant because he had been faithful in the small areas of life.

When God was bringing David into the public place, before killing Goliath he had to face the ridicule of his own brothers. They mocked him. They tried to send him back to the sheep. But he knew they were not his enemies; Goliath was. He didn't waste time arguing with his brothers—he had something much more important to face.

Then he had to overcome King Saul's opinion and suggestion to put on armor. King Saul said he couldn't go out and fight the giant without proper armor. But Saul's armor didn't fit. It hindered David more than helped him. So the only thing he faced Goliath with was a sling and five smooth stones, along with the help of the Holy Spirit. With these he was able to kill the enemy.

Now I know that many of you are ready to defeat the enemy as you are about to get the breakthrough. You can't wait an extra hour. But be careful at this point because that is when temptation will present itself. Some of you may have already given in to temptation. But know this: it's not too late! If you have fallen away, God will forgive you as you repent. Jesus' blood is still powerful to cleanse you and make you whole.

How Demons Attack People

When I was in college in the city of Hubli, I used to go outside of the house during the night and to pray. Sometimes I used to walk and pray, and other times I would just sit on the steps of the stores which were closed. One night not a single person was in sight. Suddenly, I saw two people walking and talking on the other side of the road. I had no idea what they were talking about. But I suddenly could see a third person appear on the road and then quickly disappear. It was a dark figure. I couldn't believe my eyes. After a minute I could see another dark figure walking down the street. It came up to one of the two men and began to hold him. The dark figure held the person, he suddenly became very aggressive and started kicking the other person. God was showing me how demons influence people. From that point on I learned about how demons influence people. John 10:10 says, "The thief cometh not, but for to steal, and to kill, and to destroy: I am come that they might have life, and that they might have it more abundantly."

Temptations

Demonic spirits can trap men and women with lust and deceive many. Often when you are around a man or woman who is bound by these types of demons, you feel very attracted and may feel sexually aroused by them. By their talk and the spirit behind them, you can fall into that particular sin.

This can happen as you pass through certain streets in a town too. If a town is influenced by prostitution or adultery, let's say, then you may begin to feel emotionally disturbed in these areas. Some say they even have sexual dreams while staying in those places. This is because those particular spirits heavily affect that area. It is important for you to stay in the presence of God and stay connected to a good church. When people are attacked by these spirits, if they don't spiritually clean themselves immediately, then those spirits will begin to build strongholds in their minds. They will slowly begin to slide into pornography, masturbation, or try to get a partner to fulfill their lust.

Even when you come across certain people you don't know, you feel drawn towards them. Proverbs reminds us to be careful in the presence of a deceitful woman. She can trap you by her words. Joseph had to run away without his garment because a married woman continually tried to tempt him to sleep with her. It would do us well to do the same thing. If there is a specific place which always pulls us down into these kinds of temptations, then we should stay away from that place.

There were some nurses who came for prayer once and said that when they are working in the hospital, the doctors would force them to have sex with them. They were carrying shame because they were forced to do that. They wanted to be free, but were stuck. Many of you are working in different places where a person may be trying to ruin your life. It is important to please God by staying holy. Find someone, talk to them about what is going on, and have them pray for you.

Demons Build Strongholds

Demons often attach themselves to books, trees, dolls (voodoo practicing people), certain types of brass shaped objects (Freemasons), or various other objects (New Age people use different types of objects as well). People will often speak curses over these objects, and then there is demonic influence in others' houses because of the object residing in that house.

There was a particular object that disturbed me a lot when I was in someone's house a while ago. When I was praying in that room, I saw a demon coming out of an object on their shelf. I asked my friend how they got it. And they told me that one of their friend's gave it to them, but that person was heavily involved in New Age. Then it completely made sense why I saw that demon coming out of it.

Another family was going through a very difficult time. There was a lot of sickness and accidents; their house was even broken into. When they asked me to come and pray, God showed me about witchcraft that was present, as well as certain objects in their house that were dedicated to demons. The family brought out some expensive brass object when I told them what God had shown me. They said that these were the objects that were used by their forefathers for witchcraft and Freemasonry. They had cleaned it, but just kept it in their home because it was a very expensive item. I told them that they had to throw it away because it belonged to the devil and was once dedicated to demons.

Once people get free from witchcraft and Freemasonry, they should throw away all the material and objects belonging to those practices or used in them. They need to be sanctified by the blood of Jesus—in fact, everything that belongs to them needs to be sanctified.

I was staying at another person's house, and after everyone had gone to bed, I went outside and began praying among some trees. God opened my eyes to see demons hanging around everywhere on the trees. I didn't understand why I was seeing that in this particular area. So the next day I asked this family about the history of the area, particularly where the trees were. They told me that area was used in World War II; they had buried many soldiers there whom they did not recognize. But after many years people began building and using that place. I then knew why it was so affected by demons.

Mediums

In Leviticus 20:22 and Deuteronomy 18:11 the Bible strictly speaks against consulting dead people, or communicating with spirits. King Saul disobeyed God by going to see a witch, seeing if he could communicate with Samuel, who was dead (1 Samuel 28:13). He had sinned against God and David was being raised up to take his place as King of Israel. So Saul went to inquire of the dead, which is very dangerous. People do this even today and get into bondage from it. They get connected with familiar spirits, which will communicate with them.

Familiar spirits deceive people. As I minister in different places around the world, though people say they are Christians, they are not completely delivered yet from these familiar spirits. They still get some information from them, both deceiving themselves and others. That is why discernment is so important for the people of God.

The simplest way to discern is through sensing in your spirit whether something is good or bad—you feel disturbed when you come into contact with such people. If you don't feel good about someone, don't allow them to lay hands upon you. It is good if they don't speak false prophecy over you. If this has already happened to you, Jesus can set you free. He is greater than every negative word spoken over you.

The discerning of the spirits is mentioned in 1 Corinthians 12:10, "To another the working of miracles; to another prophecy; to another discerning of spirits; to another divers kinds of tongues; to another the interpretation of tongues." It is a gift of the Holy Spirit given to the believer to be able to distinguish the presence of good and bad spirits—of angelic and demonic, of God and that of the devil.

Luke tells the story of a young woman, possessed by demons, who followed Paul and him, proclaiming they were servants of God.

> And it came to pass, as we went to prayer, a certain damsel possessed with a spirit of divination met us, which brought her masters much gain by soothsaying: The same followed Paul and us, and cried, saying, These men are the servants of the most high God, which shew unto us the way of salvation. And this did she many days. But Paul, being grieved, turned and said to the spirit, I command thee in the name of Jesus Christ to come out of her. And he came out the same hour. — Acts 16:16-18

A spirit of divination possessed this woman, enabling her to bring her masters money through fortunetelling. After following Paul and Luke around for some time, Paul began to be grieved. Even though this happened for many days, he waited for just the right time when the anointing and gift of discernment was operating within him. Then, when the anointing was present, he cast the demon out and she was instantly delivered.

When God opens our eyes by the gift of discernment and the anointing of the Holy Spirit, He will also give us the power, strength, and faith to break the stronghold. The demonic power and stronghold will be immediately broken as we pray against it. Sometimes when I pray for somebody who is either sick, or on their deathbed, God shows me what the cause is through discernment. When I cast that spirit out, they are immediately delivered or healed. This even happens in certain physical locations where a stronghold has been set up—God shows me through the power of the Holy Spirit and through the name of Jesus how to break it. Those physical locations can be cleansed.

When the gift of discernment is in operation, we will also see angels assisting us, not just the bad spirits. One time I was in India having a seminar on the Holy Spirit. On the last day of the meeting, there was such an outpouring of the Holy Spirit taking place. As I was ministering to the people, they were falling under the power of God. They were unable to stand. A family was there who were not Christians. They brought with them a lady who was possessed by many demons. As she was in the crowd, the demon began manifesting with hissing sounds and evil facial expressions. I thought of going and praying for her, but the Holy Spirit immediately told me that it wasn't the time. The enemy was only trying to distract the meeting. So I just told them that they would have to wait.

The family and some of the leaders were upset that I didn't immediately pray for her. I kept ministering to everyone present as the power of God was evident. I prayed for the last person there when the Holy Spirit told me that it was now time to command the demons to leave that woman. People had been holding the woman the entire time I was ministering to everyone else. She suddenly became very aggressive and ran towards me. The Holy Spirit was already there and I knew He was in control of the situation. I said, "Jesus" as the woman, who was rushing towards me, fell to the ground. All the demons left at that moment, without me doing anything further. It was so powerful! It is good to be sensitive to the Holy Spirit because He moves differently every time.

A few years ago I went to a place called Mysore, India, to minister to a few people. After a few days I traveled to North India. While there, God brought me back to Mysore in the Spirit. He showed me a man whom I met earlier and was supposedly a very good Christian. When I began to pray for him, I saw his face turn ugly as the demons began to manifest. I did not know until then that this man was possessed. So I spent some time praying for him until I felt a release from God.

Buses And Planes

When I travel on a bus, a train, or a plane after some powerful meetings, demonized people will have trouble sitting next to me because of the presence of God. One time my friend was sitting next to me and on the other side there was a demon possessed man. When I started gently speaking in tongues and praising God, that man started to fall down in the bus and began manifesting. My friend told me to stop praying. The demonized man couldn't sit down unless I stopped praying.

There have been several times a similar thing has happened in the plane. After some powerful meetings in England, I was sitting in the plane where there were three seats in a row. One seat was vacant. A man came and sat next to me, but he couldn't sit for too long. He started jumping and losing control. He then left that seat and went to sit in another seat far away from me because of the anointing of God that had been present.

Another time a woman came and sat next to me on the plane. God immediately showed me that she was a Satanist. When we began to talk with each other, I asked her who she was. Without any hesitation she told me that she was a Satanist. I was able to share the gospel with her during that plane ride. Nothing visible happened, but I know God's Word is powerful and able to pierce the hardest of hearts.

I was praying and interceding in Pittsburgh, Pennsylvania, in 2010. God took me to India in the Spirit where I was watching a man involved in different activities that God was asking me to pray for. There was a terrible odor around him when I went near him, which I could not bear to smell. I was puzzled about why this man smelled so bad. As I continued to pray a demon began to manifest in him. After a couple of days I called his friends and tried to find out about who this man was. The people told me he had been initially good but later on began to fight and argue with different people. He hated a certain family and wanted to do bad things to them. He went to the demons and tried witchcraft so he could harm them. He was then possessed and almost died. However, God still loved him and wanted to bring him back.

God will use you to help others and to change the circumstances they are in, helping them be saved from accidents and even death. God has shown me many times to pray in the spirit for people who are in their last stages of life, and then they were suddenly taken out of danger and their lives were restored.

Angel Of God's Visitation

I have had many experiences with the angels of God as I give myself to prayer. There was a time my friend called me to ask if I could pray for a woman in his family. So I agreed to join him in prayer. It was evening when we went to pray for her and several people from the family were already there as we arrived. My friend introduced me to all of them and then they told me who I was to pray for. She was close to six feet tall with a big build. Instead of allowing me to pray right away, everyone kept talking for close to an hour. I didn't know what to do, so I gently started praying in the spirit with my head down. I then began to strongly feel the presence of God upon me. Out of the corner of my eye, I saw that a cloud began to come into the house. There was an angel of God. I felt as if I needed to pray for this woman in that moment. So in the midst of deep conversations taking place, in the boldness of God I told her we needed to pray now. They couldn't believe that I would interrupt like this.

So everyone around became quiet as I began to pray for this woman. When I went to pray for her, she immediately stood up and then fell back in the chair. The family thought she had fainted. But I knew the Holy Spirit touched her and demonic spirits left her. She opened her eyes and I felt like my friend and I were to leave and go back home.

When we left that place I went back to my room and my friend went back to his house. The next day he called me and said he wanted to meet; it was urgent. He told me that he needed to confess something before me. He said, "I didn't tell you that this woman was possessed with demons. Many people came to pray for her earlier; and she became so aggressive and overtook the pastors and preachers who came to pray for her. She had beaten them up. I didn't want to tell you beforehand because I didn't want to scare you about the woman. But the family had told me after we left the house what had happened."

He continued, "The demons came upon her when you went to pray for her; that is why she stood up, tried to scream, and lifted her hand against you. But she saw the angel that was standing in the corner immediately come over and slap her face and all the demons left her. She also became dumb for two hours afterwards—she was stuck on the chair for two hours without uttering any speech. After that she became totally normal and was totally delivered." Praise God for that deliverance!

When angels show up in meetings, the demons are in big trouble. The angels accompanying us are the promise of God out of His Word (Psalm 91). Be obedient to God's Word and the angels will always accompany you, bringing protection for you.

I will often see angels as I travel because they have come to protect me. They are always watching over us. When we stay in faith and in the Word of God, according to Psalm 103:20, the angels will be excelled and activated on our behalf. That means they will really protect us and help us in whatever situation we find ourselves.

God promises to send His angels to keep charge over us and to watch us (Psalm 91). We see many times throughout the Bible that God and angels fight against the enemies of Israel. We hear about angels in the New Testament as well. They do many different jobs to help the body of Christ. An angel of the Lord opened the prison door and delivered Peter (Acts 12). An angel of the Lord appeared to Paul in a boat, comforting him and causing hope to spring up in his heart that everyone would be safe (Acts 27). And in Daniel's time we see angels bringing messages from God, first having to fight against territorial spirits (the king of Persia) before God's people received the answer (Daniel 10).

I was teaching in Bible School for a whole week in Holland, Sweden. I felt like I was to talk to the dean of the school about arranging a special evening meeting for all the schools. They said that no one would attend because most of the students were always tired; only a few would show up. And if a few did show up, they would not stay more than an hour. But because I insisted, the dean announced that a special meeting would be held.

The chapel was completely packed with all the students who attended. They began to receive healing as I started preaching. There was a boy who had a small growth on his foot and he felt heat on it as I prayed for him. When I asked him to remove his socks and shoes, he was utterly shocked because the growth had disappeared.

After seeing some more healings take place, I felt led to pray for everyone present. So I had all the students stand up and told everyone to praise and worship God. Then I told them to be very quiet after a few minutes. I was also standing up and waiting on God along with them. I suddenly felt wind rushing all around as my eyes opened up. The room was being opened up to the spirit realm. An angel of the Lord was coming down as I began to lose control of the meeting and everyone around began to fall down under the power of God. People were crying and being touched by the Holy Spirit. I was watching the angel walk through the crowd touching people. The Spirit of God told me to follow him and touch those he touches. As I was touching the people, they were experiencing the mighty power of God and fell on the floor.

There was a notorious popular girl at that school. She was sitting at the last seat towards the end of the hall. The angel walked all the way through the isle, straight to her. He had a golden jar, took something out of it, and began to give it to her. God prompted me to lay hands on her as the angel was giving her the jar. When I laid hands on her, she started shaking and screaming so loudly and she fell down under the power of the Holy Spirit. When everything was over, everybody in the hall wanted to know what had happened to her. Still crying, she told us when the meeting was over that she had seen exactly what I had seen. She pointed to the place the angel had descended and where he had went. She saw him walk over to her and touch her. He gave her particular gifts of the Holy Spirit. It was a very powerful experience and the whole school was blessed. From the very next day, God started powerfully using her with the word of knowledge, wisdom, and the prophetic gifts, which was really amazing. Man looks at the outward appearances but God looks at the heart. God truly blessed the entire school with His anointing!

Long ago I was praying and seeking God for an answer to one of my prayers. After praying for a few days, I was praying in my room during the night when I felt like I was to stand up, lifting my hands to God in worship. I began to confess that Jesus is Lord and said, "Thank You, Jesus, for being with me. Thank You, for Your presence." As I continued to praise God, I saw a mist enter my room and felt warmth come into my hands and feet. I didn't know what was happening. I checked everything to make sure I was all right. But I continued to worship God even though I was wondering what was happening to me. Suddenly, two angels descended into my room. I wasn't sure why there were two of them, but one of them spoke to me and then immediately left. I was fully charged by the presence of God. I felt such an ecstasy and joy at their presence and at what they had spoken to me! Such a deep peace moved into my heart. It was absolutely amazing. It is important to continue to stay in the presence of God and worshipping Jesus.

There was another time I had an open air crusade in an interior Indian village. There were about a thousand people there even though there was no form of transportation. The history of the village was that they were heavily involved in witchcraft and voodoo. They would send demons against each other to kill people. An entire village vanished because of this. This was the first meeting where the people saw the power of God being visibly demonstrated. Many were being healed. One of the most amazing things of the meeting was that the majority of the people in attendance were demon possessed. Every day, because of the presence of Jesus, many people would fall and manifest as the demons left them. Almost everyone was delivered by the third day, at which our last meeting finished at about four in the morning.

There was a couple who came with their twenty-year-old daughter. They were very sad because their daughter was the only one not delivered from the demons that had been tormenting her; the whole town was delivered, just not her. As they came closer, the young girl fell down on the ground and began to roll around very fast. Naturally, this wouldn't have been possible. As soon as she found a stone or a rock, she would bang her head against it. Her head was moving so fast! Some of our volunteers caught her and brought her to me to pray. It was very difficult for five or six strong men to restrain her.

The Holy Spirit spoke to my heart when I began to pray, telling me not to pray for her because her parents were lying and they still had a lot of witchcraft. I asked if they had anything associated with witchcraft in their home or on the young daughter. They said they didn't. Then I told them that I couldn't pray for them. Some of the leaders in the town were not happy because I didn't pray for her right then.

But the very next day we were invited to go to the house of one of the main people of the town for breakfast. As we were walking by, I felt to turn on the roadside. As I did, somebody was standing there—that same young girl from the day before. As soon as I looked into her eyes, she fell down and began to manifest. The parents requested that I come to their home to pray more for this girl. The Holy Spirit led me to go to their home.

As I was standing and praying in their house, the Holy Spirit instructed me that they had something hidden in their house that was associated with witchcraft. They were so afraid as I revealed this and they pointed out the four corners of the house. Our friends, who were volunteers, dug up each of the four corners of the house and found four pots filled with all kinds of demonic things. We burnt them, renounced them, and broke all the powers of the devil over their home. We broke the link in the name of Jesus and the young girl was totally delivered. They were shocked at what God had done for them.

Then the whole town came to meet with us. They said this girl was well known to everyone, and they all knew how possessed she was. They had spent a lot of money taking her everywhere to get her help, but nothing would work. Only Jesus could deliver her. They had us stay an extra day and threw a party for us. It was amazing to see the blessing of God on the town after the meetings!

All of these stories took place because we were sensitive to the Holy Spirit and were able to discern what it was we were to do. I really praise God for His power! It is greater than anything!

CHAPTER 9

Undoing All The Wrong Things

The first step in breaking strongholds is to ask God's forgiveness in Jesus' name for doing what was wrong and by wrongly using the senses. Ask Him to cleanse you with His blood. If fear, worries, or any other strongholds have caused you to behave abnormally, other than understanding that you're God's child, you need to change your thinking, talking, hearing, and your looking. Then also confess to Jesus and say, "From now on I am going to change my bad behavior. I need Your strength to help me do this. I'm Your child and washed by the blood of Jesus. You are in me. My body is the temple of God (1 Corinthians 3:16). God, You are greater than all of my problems (1 John 4:4). Now I stand as a child of God on the authority of Jesus by the Word of God. I cast down all the wrong imaginations, fears, and worries. I break them in the name of Jesus."

Use God's authority and break each stronghold in Jesus' name. Then confess again that you are washed by the blood of Jesus and have the peace of God because the Prince of Peace is within you. "God hath not given us the spirit of fear; but of power, and of love, and of a sound mind" (2 Timothy 1:7). Confessing God's Word and believing what it says concerning you will help you to demolish the strongholds in your mind.

Watching horror movies will many times cause those images to stay in your mind for days at a time. It is good to completely avoid such things. When those horror movies create fear, it may become a stronghold until you break it through the authority of the Word as well as by the anointing of the Holy Spirit. But if you engage in singing, praising God, and worshipping Jesus, it will help you to stay in the presence of God and avoid such things.

If you know some genuine men of God, who are filled with the Holy Spirit and walk in the authority of God, those people can also pray with you and break those strongholds off your mind. The anointing they carry is powerful enough to break the strongholds and set you free. Another simple step is to pray in tongues, worshipping God, and claiming all the promises of God for yourself.

CHAPTER 10

Extraordinary Power From Above To Overcome

Paul instructs us, "Finally, my brethren, be strong in the Lord, and in the power of his might. Put on the whole armor of God, that ye may be able to stand against the wiles of the devil" (Ephesians 6:10-11). Being strong in the Lord and protected by Him will help us win the battle we are in.

Jesus has given us two kinds of power. The first is that He has given us power (or authority) to become children of God. John 1:12 says, "But as many as received him, to them gave he power to become the sons of God, even to them that believe on his name." Secondly, Jesus gave us power over the devil: "Behold, I give unto you power to tread on serpents and scorpions, and over all the power of the enemy: and nothing shall by any means hurt you" (Luke 10:19). To all those who receive Jesus as their Lord, He gives them the authority, right, liberty, and strength to be children of God. And He has also given us authority, right, liberty, and power to trample on Satan. The kingdom of Satan is under our jurisdiction—we have legal power to bruise his head.

One of the purposes for Jesus coming into the world was not only to give us eternal life by dying on the cross, but also to destroy the work of the devil. First John 3:8 says, "For this purpose the Son of God was manifested, that He might destroy the works of the devil." And Acts 10:38 says, "How God anointed Jesus of Nazareth with the Holy Ghost and with power: who went about doing good, and healing all that were oppressed of the devil; for God was with him." It is important to note that Jesus, with the power of the Holy Spirit, went about doing good and healing all those who were oppressed by the enemy.

The power to trample on the devil is the result of the power of being the children of God. Without being God's children, we cannot have authority over the enemy. If we are washed by the blood of Jesus and filled with the Holy Spirit, then we have power over every work of Satan. "And the God of peace shall bruise Satan under your feet shortly. The grace of our Lord Jesus Christ be with you. Amen," Paul wrote to the Romans (Romans 16:20).

James reminds us, "Submit yourselves therefore to God. Resist the devil, and he will flee from you" (James 4:7). We need to understand how great and powerful God is. Once we understand how powerful He is, then we will begin to understand the full extent of His power within us by becoming His children. The people who know "their God shall be strong, and do exploits" for Him (Daniel 11:32). We are God's temple and the Spirit of God, who has all power and authority, lives within us: "Know ye not that ye are the temple of God, and that the Spirit of God dwelleth in you?" (1 Corinthians 3:16). And John reminds us: "Ye are of God, little children, and have overcome them: because greater is he that is in you, than he that is in the world" (1 John 4:4).

Being In The Body Of Christ

God made a pattern for the tabernacle and revealed it to Moses, which would be a type of the church, the body of Christ. Psalm 133 declares:

Behold, how good and how pleasant it is for brethren to dwell together in unity! It is like the precious ointment upon the head, that ran down upon the beard, even Aaron's beard: that went down to the skirts of his garments; As the dew of Hermon, and as the dew that descended upon the mountains of Zion: for there the LORD commanded the blessing, even life for evermore.

Paul builds upon this revelation of the church being likened to the tabernacle when he explains how we all work together: "In whom all the building fitly framed together groweth unto an holy temple in the Lord: In whom ye also are builded together for an habitation of God through the Spirit" (Ephesians 2:21-22).

When we dwell together in unity, with one mind and with one spirit, agreeing on the truth with one another in the name of Jesus, the greatest power will there be released. If the church really understands this truth, it will shake nations. "How should one chase a thousand, and two put ten thousand to flight, except their Rock had sold them, and the LORD had shut them up?" (Deuteronomy 32:30).

God pours out His powerful anointing on His body, of which He is the head. There is nothing else other than the body of Christ in which everything the enemy brings against us can be crushed. Paul writes,

And what is the exceeding greatness of his power to us-ward who believe, according to the working of his mighty power, Which he wrought in Christ, when he raised him from the dead, and set him at his own right hand in the heavenly places, **Far above all principality, and power, and might, and dominion, and every name that is named, not only in this world, but also in that which is to come: And hath put all things under his feet, and gave him to be the head over all things to the church, Which is his body, the fulness of him that filleth all in all.** — Ephesians 1:19-23, emphasis mine

Furthermore, Paul writes, "For in him dwelleth all the fulness of the Godhead bodily. And ye are complete in him, which is the head of all principality and power" (Colossians 2:9-10). Since God has placed His greatest power in His body, we can be plugged into the fullness of His creative power by being in the body of Christ, with Jesus being our head. Then the synergy of the body and the power of the Spirit will begin to operate through us — we will put ten thousand to flight because we're part of the body of Christ. There is nothing compared to this power on the face of the earth.

Paul tells the Ephesians that the purpose of this mystery of the people of God being His body was to

> bring to light what is the administration of the mystery which for ages has been hidden in God who created all things; so that the manifold wisdom of God might now be made known through the church to the rulers and the authorities in the heavenly places. This was in accordance with the eternal purpose which He carried out in Christ Jesus our Lord, in whom we have boldness and confident access through faith in Him. — Ephesians 3:9-12, NASB, emphasis mine

God's fullness dwells in Jesus as well as the body of Christ. There are no limits to His power, for it is exceedingly great (Ephesians 1:19).

Misunderstanding The Power

Many believing Christians misunderstand what God has done for them through Jesus Christ. Because of this misunderstanding, they miss out on the victory and success Jesus offers through His death and resurrection. God was pleased to come and dwell in Jesus. The fullness of the Godhead dwelt in Him, and if that same Jesus lives in us, then we have a tremendous amount of power available to us as well. The same power of the Spirit that raised Christ from the dead now lives in everyone who has been washed by the blood of Jesus.

When Jesus died on the cross at Calvary, He took our sins, infirmities, sorrows, and pains (Isaiah 53:3-5). He also destroyed the power of Satan and made an open show of the demonic forces, having given us authority and the keys of the Kingdom. All this can be plainly seen in Paul's letter to the Colossians:

> For in him dwelleth all the fulness of the Godhead bodily. And ye are complete in him, which is the head of all principality and power: In whom also ye are circumcised with the circumcision made without hands, in putting off the body of the sins of the flesh by the circumcision of Christ: Buried with him in baptism, wherein also ye are risen with him through the faith of the operation of God, who hath raised him from the dead.
>
> And you, being dead in your sins and the uncircumcision of your flesh, hath he quickened together with him, having

forgiven you all trespasses; Blotting out the handwriting of ordinances that was against us, which was contrary to us, and took it out of the way, nailing it to his cross; And having spoiled principalities and powers, he made a shew of them openly, triumphing over them in it. — Colossians 2:9-15

It is necessary we make sure we are children of God and that He dwells within us, causing us to have the victory. We need to focus our attention completely on God instead of constantly looking at the devil. If we don't understand what God has already done for us, then we won't see success in our lives. We need to learn to live in Him. We need to learn to stay under His glory by believing His Word rather than what we feel and what the circumstances or symptoms are. Then we can properly balance knowing we are a child of God as well as knowing that the devil is under our feet through Jesus Christ.

Chapter 11

Righteousness

As we have seen in the previous chapter, it is important to know how powerful God is, both in our lives and in the world. The first step to receiving breakthrough in our life is to know how powerful and loving our God is—which means we know Him as a loving Father. For this reason it is very important to build up our relationship with our Heavenly Father. We need to draw closer to God. And if we understand the meaning of righteousness, it will help us grow much closer to Him.

The definition of righteousness is to come into His presence with boldness, without any sense of fear, guilt, shame, or condemnation. It is to come into the presence of God just as Jesus approached Him.

Many of us have a misunderstanding about the emotions of our Heavenly Father towards us. We often think He is upset with us, thus causing us to feel guilt and condemnation, which separates us from His presence.

This happened to me when I didn't receive the answer from God I desired, so I began to think that God was upset with me or maybe I wasn't walking how I should walk before Him. The enemy knows our weaknesses and tries to put the condemnation in our hearts, or he will try to remind us of our past sins which are already forgiven by God. But the Bible declares, "For as the heaven is high above the earth, so great is his mercy toward them that fear him. As far as the east is from the west, so far hath he removed our transgressions from us" (Psalm 103:11-12). When God forgives, He also forgets our sins and remembers them no more.

If there is any guilt or condemnation that comes into your heart, tell Jesus that you are sorry for committing any sin that day. This will help you to stay clean by the blood of Jesus every day. It will also enable you to walk into His presence with boldness and authority, just as Jesus walked.

I began to come into His presence this way once I understood what righteousness was and how it was given to me through the death and resurrection of Jesus Christ. Now if I feel any kind of guilt, then I will ask God to cleanse me with His blood and then walk in His righteousness.

Chapter 12

Use God's Word As A Promise

God will not do anything contrary to His Word. He will never break His promises or lie to us: "God is not a man, that he should lie; neither the son of man, that he should repent: hath he said, and shall he not do it? or hath he spoken, and shall he not make it good?" (Numbers 23:19). Furthermore, Jesus said, "Heaven and earth shall pass away, but my words shall not pass away" (Matthew 24:35). The Psalmist declared that God has even magnified His Word more than His name (Psalm 138:2). And in Joshua 1:7-8, God commands Joshua to do the following: "Only be thou strong and very courageous, that thou mayest observe to do according to all the law, which Moses my servant commanded thee: turn not from it to the right hand or to the left, that thou mayest prosper whithersoever thou goest." He then goes on to say, "This book of the law shall not depart out of thy mouth; but thou shalt meditate therein day and night, that thou mayest observe to do according to all that is written therein: for then thou shalt make thy way prosperous, and then thou shalt have good success."

God powerfully used Moses by confirming the words he spoke with powerful signs and wonders. When the Israelites arrived at the Red Sea after leaving Egypt, when there was no seemingly way out, and Pharaoh and his army was closely pursuing, the people of God cried out to Him. "And Moses said unto the people, Fear ye not, stand still, and see the salvation of the LORD, which he will shew to you to day: for the Egyptians whom ye have seen to day, ye shall see them again no more for ever. The LORD shall fight for you, and ye shall hold your peace" (Exodus 14:13-14).

Later on in the same story God told Moses to use the rod to strike the sea so it would divide. When Moses believed and obeyed what He said, they saw the miracle of the Red Sea dividing, a path being created between the waters so the Israelites could pass to the other side. It is also clear how God led the Israelites by many miracles and provided them with water and food throughout their wilderness journey. God kept them healthy for years—there was no one that even got sick among them (Psalm 105:37). He led them by a cloud by day and a pillar of fire by night.

After God used Moses to accomplish His will, then the time came for Joshua to be leader of the nation and a successor of Moses. Being trained by Moses, we learn how Joshua learned to dwell in the presence of God like Moses did. After Moses was done praying, he would go back to the camp; "but his servant Joshua, the son of Nun, a young man, departed not out of the tabernacle" (Exodus 33:11).

It is important to be filled with the Word of God, for it will help us grow and bring us to maturity. It is like a lamp unto our feet and it will direct our path (Psalm 119:105). God created the whole universe by His word—it was spoken and everything was created.

It is extremely powerful. God's Word can create our future and form our destiny. It is very important to be filled with the Word of God; for by it we protect ourselves by faith, which is produced by the Word of God. Hebrews 11 connects faith and how God created the universe by speaking. This causes me to wonder how creation takes place just by speaking. This kind of power is only released through God and His Word; therefore we need to learn how to rightly use God's Word. The writer of Hebrews speaks of faith and creation:

> Now faith is the substance of things hoped for, the evidence of things not seen. For by it the elders obtained a good report. Through faith we understand that the worlds were framed by the word of God, so that things which are seen were not made of things which do appear. By faith Abel offered unto God a more excellent sacrifice than Cain, by which he obtained witness that he was righteous, God testifying of his gifts: and by it he being dead yet speaketh. — Hebrews 11:1-4

Then Hebrews describes the miracles people saw take place because of faith. "But without faith it is impossible to please him: for he that cometh to God must believe that he is, and that he is a rewarder of them that diligently seek him" (Hebrews 11:6).

We can clearly see how the Word of God and faith operate together. God spoke and created all that we see on earth—the trees, plants, the birds, and everything around us. This same power is placed in us who have been saved and have Jesus residing in our hearts. These are the ones that are capable of doing great things for God.

It is very important to protect ourselves, our mind and our spirit man, by feeding on the Word of God every day. We need to use the shield of faith and learn that God's Word is like a sword by which we can defeat the enemy. Through these weapons we are able to oppose anything that tries to work against us and affect our mind in a negative way. Faith comes only by hearing, and hearing by God's Word, which is written in Romans 10. As we read and meditate on His Word, it creates power within us while releasing strength.

The Word of God gives us spiritual, physical, and mental strength. It is also a perfect weapon to help fight all the wrong circumstances and lies of the devil—even when the enemy places wrong symptoms in our physical bodies. We have to know and be convinced that God's Word has power to help in every area of our lives. For everyone to have success and receive God's guidance, they first must know that God's Word is true. It is powerful! Whatever God has spoken to us and whatever He has promised us, He will surely fulfill it.

The enemy speaks lies—he puts symptoms into our physical bodies and then we begin to think it is impossible to be healed. When this happens, the devil is constantly reminding us of our wrong symptoms, which we actually begin to believe to be our own. During the process, even the doctors state the problem and what is taking place in our bodies. But if we believe what God says about us, then we can receive complete healing no matter what the circumstances may be. Isaiah 53:3-5 says:

> He is despised and rejected of men; a man of sorrows, and acquainted with grief: and we hid as it were our faces from him; he was despised, and we esteemed him not. Surely he hath borne our griefs, and carried our sorrows: yet we did esteem him stricken, smitten of God, and afflicted. But he was wounded for our transgressions, he was bruised for our iniquities: the chastisement of our peace was upon him; and with his stripes we are healed.

The Word of God is powerful and gives us a life, but it is also spirit. This means that as we read, meditate upon, and speak God's Word, it creates an excellent power within us. It brings us a pathway of life to walk into the destiny and promises God has already spoken in His Word. God's Word being spirit is one of the most important aspects we need to adopt if we are going to defeat the enemy and overcome in all situations. It is vital to do this because it produces power within us.

The truth is that we are born again and receive the assurance we are children of God—we are a prophet, priest, and king. Believing this is extremely important. When the Spirit of God helps us receive the revelation of faith, it releases inside of us the strength needed to defeat the enemy. This is why it is so important to hear God's Word. Jesus said to His disciples,

> For verily I say unto you, That whosoever shall say unto this mountain, Be thou removed, and be thou cast into the sea; and shall not doubt in his heart, but shall believe that those things which he saith shall come to pass; he shall have whatsoever he saith. Therefore I say unto you, What things soever ye desire, when ye pray, believe that ye receive them, and ye shall have them. — Mark 11:23-24

When God spoke to Abraham, God told him that he would have a son. Although Abraham had many chances to doubt God, he did not. He chose to believe and trust that what God said, He would do. Paul explains it this way:

(As it is written, I have made thee a father of many nations,) before him whom he believed, even God, who quickeneth the dead, and calleth those things which be not as though they were. Who against hope believed in hope, that he might become the father of many nations, according to that which was spoken, So shall thy seed be. And being not weak in faith, he considered not his own body now dead, when he was about an hundred years old, neither yet the deadness of Sarah's womb: He staggered not at the promise of God through unbelief; but was strong in faith, giving glory to God; And being fully persuaded that, what he had promised, he was able also to perform. And therefore it was imputed to him for righteousness. — Romans 4:12-22

Abraham experienced all types of feelings and symptoms in light of what God spoke. Naturally he could not bear or produce any child on his own. By having seen all of these physical setbacks, he did not doubt or give any chance for these thoughts to cause him to waver, but began to believe God's Word. Instead of complaining about his age and physical body, he kept praising and glorifying God. This was his key for receiving his miracle as well the fulfillment of the

Word of God. He was strong in faith and believed what God had said. And this pleased God.

It is impossible to please God without faith. Faith must be present if we're going to see God's mighty promises come to pass in our lives. With all of the trials, temptations, and bad situations taking place around us, we need to believe and hold fast to what God has promised us, just like Abraham did. Although you may go through difficult circumstances or have physical symptoms in your body, you ought to focus on what the promise of God is for you in that situation. Hold on to that promise more than the circumstances you can see with your natural eyes. Believe and speak God's Word over your situation and you will see things change.

We should be very careful not to bind ourselves by negative words and say the wrong things when speaking. When God promises something in His Word, He will keep His promise no matter what. Proverbs 18:21 says, "Death and life are in the power of the tongue." Because of this, we need to release life when we speak—speaking the life found in the Word of God.

After you have been washed by the blood of Jesus and have Him in your heart, you have become a special person. You have become the temple of God, part of the holy generation, and a royal priesthood. When the Word of God declares your identity in Christ and who are you becoming in the future, you need to see yourself how God sees you and declare it boldly. You will then speak, live, and see this in your inner man. This produces the reality in your life to overcome every situation and break every stronghold. You must agree and say with your mouth: "I am a child of God. I have been washed by the blood of Jesus. I am the temple of God. I am a priest and king." You can say all these things because of the one who lives in you!

Chapter 13

Reading And Meditating

God commands us to not only read the Word of God, but also to meditate deeply upon it. Meditation brings a picture of what we are reading. It causes us to think deeply, to mull over, and to apply to our lives what God's Word is speaking to us. Meditation takes God's Word from information to revelation.

The Psalmist speaks of the man who is blessed because he meditates on God's Word day and night: "Blessed is the man that walketh not in the counsel of the ungodly, nor standeth in the way of sinners, nor sitteth in the seat of the scornful. But his delight is in the law of the LORD; and in his law doth he meditate day and night" (Psalm 1:1-2). Furthermore, we will be like a tree planted by rivers of water that bears fruit all year long. We will be successful in all our ways and we'll prosper in everything we do because we know how to meditate.

Paul describes us as "the temple of God" (1 Corinthians 3:16). When we begin to meditate on those words, our thinking turns into a picture screen. Our imagination begins to show us that we are the temple of God and that God dwells inside our body. The temple in which God lives will be holy, clean, and strong. Just like God's glory covered the temple in the Old Testament, so meditating on this reveals the picture of God's glory being inside of us, as well as outwardly enveloping us. Holding this vision before us will produce strength and power, both of which are important to maturity in Christ.

A similar reaction takes place as we meditate on 1 Peter 2:9: "But ye are a chosen generation, a royal priesthood, an holy nation, a peculiar people; that ye should shew forth the praises of him who hath called you out of darkness into his marvelous light." When we meditate on this Scripture, we actually begin to believe we are a royal priesthood, a holy nation, and a peculiar people. We believe that God actually chose us to show forth His praises as He called us out of darkness and into His light. Meditation let's God's Word get deep down inside of us, changing our heart and life because the Word of God abides in us.

Many times we depend upon the five senses rather than believe God and His Word. Faith is not a feeling. Faith and fear will never work together. When people hear bad news or certain loud sounds, fear is the first thing that begins to attack them. Without knowing the facts, many of us become afraid because of the lies the enemy puts into our minds.

Sometimes people have a spirit of fear, anger, or other types of spirits that are holding their mind in captivity. These spirits (strongholds) continually control people and make them believe the wrong ideas, contrary to what God says. The stronghold in their mind is the same one that will always control them and make them behave in different ways. God made us all in His image as sons and daughters of God. That is why it is very important that we should constantly renew our mind with the Word of God and pray in the spirit. We also need to walk in *shalom*, the peace of God—where nothing is missing and nothing is broken. With all of this we need to keep the joy of God so we can overcome everything the enemy has tried to put in our mind.

Let us remember who we are in Christ Jesus. First John 4:4 says that "greater is he that is in you, than he that is in the world." No evil will befall us neither shall any plague come near our dwelling only because we belong to Jesus. We will be considered a child of the King. Though we live on earth, we also are part of another kingdom at the very same time. That kingdom is the Kingdom of God. God and His angels are always protecting us when we hold onto His Word and trust Him at all times. He promised that He would never leave us nor forsake us (Hebrews 13:5).

There is always power and help released when we stand on and believe His Word. It is important to speak out loud, with our mouth, what the Bible says about us. Not only that, but we must also believe what we say about ourselves. What we believe about ourselves, we will see it and then begin to worship God, rejoicing in what has come to pass.

Knowing what the Bible says about us and who we are in Christ Jesus is important if we are to fulfill the plans and purposes of God. So continually read the Word of God, meditating deeply on it. Then you will speak the Word so that you will see the fulfillment of it.

Many times we always try to sense something or see something with our natural eyes before believing it. The faith we have in God can change the entire circumstance we are in. When doctors give up, God can do the rest. When it is impossible with man, it is possible with God. When we hold onto His Word and believe what we've prayed and declared, then it will come to pass. God is faithful and will always do what He promises!

Chapter 14

What You See Can Be Yours

Genesis tells the story of Abraham receiving the promise from God that he would be the father of many nations. Genesis 15:5 says, "And (God) brought (Abraham) forth abroad, and said, Look now toward heaven, and tell the stars, if thou be able to number them: and he said unto him, So shall thy seed be." When Abraham was very old, he was living in his tent and traveling around the countryside. One night God came and asked him to come out and look at the sky, to see if he could count the stars. God told him, as Abraham stood gazing up towards Heaven, that what he was looking at was going to be his future. As many as the stars in Heaven in multitude, that is how many of Abraham's decedents there was going to be. God had to bring him out of his own thinking and limitations in order to bring him to another place where he could see his future and blessings through God's eyes. "And he believed in the LORD; and he counted it to him for righteousness" (Genesis 15:6).

Jacob, though God had already blessed him and promised to do so more, saw a vision of a ladder with angels of God ascending and descending it. After this vision, he went to live with his uncle Laben, who cheated him and deceived him. In the midst of all of these tough circumstances, God gave Jacob wisdom. So Jacob said to Laben, "You have been blessed. I don't have anything that belongs to you. Whatever the goats give birth to next, whether they are spotted and speckled, that will be my salary." Genesis then tells the story:

> And Jacob took him rods of green poplar, and of the hazel and chestnut tree; and pilled white stakes in them, and made the white appear which was in the rods. He set the rods which he had pilled before the flocks in the gutters in the watering troughs when the flocks came to drink, that they should conceive when they came to drink. The flocks conceived before the rods, and brought forth cattle ringstraked, speckled, and spotted. — Genesis 30:37-39

The flocks conceived and gave birth to what they saw. Genesis 30:43 sums up Jacob's life: "And the man increased exceedingly, and had much cattle, and maidservants, and menservants, and camels, and asses."

When we are born again (receive Jesus as our Lord and Savior), we become a new creation. Paul says that "if any man be in Christ, he is a new creature: old things are passed away; behold, all things are become new" (2 Corinthians 5:17). Our spirit man, which was once dead, is made active and alive in Christ. The spirit man is then able to see, hear, and sense what is taking place all around.

Jesus talks about hearing and seeing throughout the Gospels. Paul also prays for us in Ephesians 1:17-18, "That the God of our Lord Jesus Christ, the Father of glory, may give unto you the spirit of wisdom and revelation in the knowledge of him: The eyes of your understanding being enlightened; that ye may know what is the hope of his calling, and what the riches of the glory of his inheritance in the saints." Paul was praying for the spirit of wisdom, revelation, and knowledge of God so that our eyes of understanding would be open. We would then be able to grasp what all the riches of the glory of God's inheritance is, which He has given to us. We can inherit them and we can walk into them.

Mark reflects on the life of Jesus as He talked about seeing spiritual truths, or seeing in the spirit, or our eyes being open (Mark 4:9; 8:17-18). Sometimes Jesus says, "Are you still blind that you can't see?" Other times He asked, "Are you still deaf that you can't hear?" And after Jesus was resurrected, He joined two disciples on the road to Emmaus, though they didn't recognize it was Jesus. He looked like a stranger to them. As He explained to them from the Prophets, Psalms, and the Law, about who He was, they felt something happening in their hearts. Thought they didn't recognize Him with their natural eyes at that moment, later their eyes were opened and they knew it was Jesus. "Then he said unto them, O fools, and slow of heart to believe all that the prophets have spoken: Ought not Christ to have suffered these things, and to enter into His glory?" (Luke 24:25-26). Then Luke further records, "And it came to pass, as he sat at meat with them, he took bread, and blessed it, and brake, and gave to them. And their eyes were opened, and they knew him; and he vanished out of their sight" (Luke 24:30-31).

After the feeding of the four thousand, Jesus told His disciples to beware of the "leaven of the Pharisees." Then reasoned among themselves because they thought He was saying it because they forgot to take bread with them. "And when Jesus knew it, He saith unto them, Why reason ye, because ye have no bread? perceive ye not, neither understand? have ye your heart yet hardened? Having eyes, see ye not? and having ears, hear ye not? and do ye not remember?" (Mark 8:17-18).

The disciples reasoned amongst themselves because they forgot to take bread with them on their journey. Jesus was upset with them and asked them if their hearts were hardened. "Don't you see? Don't you hear? Though you saw the multiplying of the bread and fish, you still don't understand? You still don't remember?" In other words, He told them that they still doubted what He could do through them. Again, this is not perceiving and seeing with natural eyes, but with the eyes of their spirits. In all of these Scriptures about believing, seeing, hearing, and understanding, it is referring to the spiritual senses, not the natural. This all happens in the spiritual realm.

We've been studying about our spirit man who sees, hears, and understands things in the realm of the spirit. At the same time, when our spiritual senses begin to operate, we can see through our natural eyes and hear through our natural ears what is happening in the spiritual realm. We begin to physically see spiritual things and audibly hear spiritual things.

When we are born again, our spirit man always wants to follow God and His Spirit. The spirit man gets strengthened during worship, reading the Bible, and by praying in the spirit. So, when we feed our spirit man, he grows stronger and bigger, ever longing more and more after God and His ways.

When we begin to see, hear, and sense in the spiritual realm, that is a big key to operating successfully in the natural realm. When God says something about us, we hold onto that, seeing and believing what He said to be true, then those things will come to pass. God fulfills the desire of the righteous.

Elisha desired the double portion of the Holy Spirit which was upon Elijah, and God gave it to him. When Elisha asked his master about the double portion of anointing, Elijah said he would only receive it if he saw him taken up into Heaven. Elisha focused on his master and ended up getting what he desired. And the Scriptures record twice as many miracles in the life of Elisha than took place in Elijah's life.

"Now unto him that is able to do exceeding abundantly above all that we ask or think, according to the power that worketh in us, Unto him be glory in the church by Christ Jesus throughout all ages, world without end. Amen" (Ephesians 3:20-21). God can do more than we could ask or possibly think. When we even think or imagine about our future, God can see it and He can give it to you. It is good to desire more from God.

CHAPTER 15

Faith

Faith is not a feeling. In fact, faith and fear are completely opposite. If we say that we have faith, we cannot work with fear. Fear contaminates faith. It can try to limit and restrict the faith we possess. People will sometimes say, "I hope I can see my healing." Hope is always future, but faith is now. Hebrews 11:1 says, "Now faith is the substance of things hoped for, the evidence of things not seen."

When we pray for our healing, faith brings confidence and will give us a substance of the healing, which we are supposed to receive. Hope means we're longing for something in the future while faith brings the future into the present. Since the Bible declares that we are healed by His stripes (Isaiah 53:5), then we are already healed by faith. This is a past tense statement. It means that Jesus has already bore our sickness in His own body on the tree—we are already healed.

You may ask me, "How can you say that when I have physical symptoms and real pain?" Faith believes in our heart that what Christ has done for us is settled. It doesn't depend upon our five senses. Our senses (seeing, hearing, smelling, tasting, touching, feeling) will notify us of the feelings we're experiencing, or the differing kinds of symptoms or pains we have. But according to the Bible those symptoms cannot stand before God's Word mixed with faith. Jesus declared how powerful faith truly is:

> For verily I say unto you, That whosoever shall say unto this mountain, Be thou removed, and be thou cast into the sea; and shall not doubt in his heart, but shall believe that those things which he saith shall come to pass; he shall have whatsoever he saith. Therefore I say unto you, What things soever ye desire, when ye pray, believe that ye receive them, and ye shall have them. — Mark 11:23-24

When we believe God's Word, according to Hebrews 11:1, Mark 11:23-24, and Romans 4:17-20, we will see miracles happen. When we believe that Jesus has taken our sicknesses, this belief can give us the completeness of healing, which is God's will that we should be complete in Him. The same happens when we speak out of our mouth the faith that resides in our heart. When we pray, believe that we have received what we are asking for and we shall have it. If we believe and see ourselves as completely and healthy in Him, then we shall see it. When we hold onto that, praising and worshipping God without any fear, guilt, or condemnation, then we will see it manifested in the natural world. Our senses will feel differently as we stand in faith that Jesus has bore our sicknesses.

Abraham felt and saw everything contrary to the promise of God. His body was old. He felt physically weak. His wife was old and past childbearing age. He had thoughts that his body would not produce a child. But instead of focusing on these outward circumstances, he believed God's promise that he would have a child. Faith never gave any chance for the circumstance or symptoms to speak to him. He kept giving glory to God in the midst of the circumstance. He saw God's promise in his spirit and in his heart. His offspring would be like the stars of Heaven in number. Because of what he said and what he believed, it came to pass in his life. He gave birth to Isaac—meaning laughter. We may have to rejoice, praise God, and worship Him louder than the symptoms are speaking to us through your physical bodies.

Believing God is just like a man standing in front of the mirror. He will see a picture of himself; but if the man tries to reach the picture in the mirror, he cannot reach the real person there because it is just a reflection. However, the good news is that when you bring that same hand back, it can touch your real face, who is actually standing in front of the mirror. When we begin to pray and believe for a good physical condition in our body, then we focus and picture the new creation as God intended it, rather than picturing what is going wrong with our physical condition. Hold onto the healthy picture and begin to praise God, keeping that picture before you; and keep believing and praising because you will see fast results.

The Boy Who Made It

One time I went to a friend's house, who happened to live in a village, without notifying him beforehand. This family was large and very poor, but they had recently given their lives to Jesus. Everyone was sitting outside when I arrived at their house, looking very sad. So I asked them, "Why is everyone sitting outside the house?" The elderly man answered and said that one of his twin grandsons was dying. They had wrapped him in a cloth and were waiting for him to completely die. Whenever they would try to feed the baby, the milk would come out of the baby's mouth.

One of the children there brought the baby, which was wrapped in cloth, to me. I was shocked when I saw the child because it looked as if it was dead. It was very skinny. They had asked me to pray for the baby, but when I saw him, I lost all hope. I was thinking to myself that I went to see them at the wrong time. But because they asked me to pray for him, I tried to muster up some courage and began to pray in the name of Jesus: "Lord, let this boy be raised up. They have faith in You. They trust You. Lord, according to Your Word, heal this boy and raise this boy." After I was done praying I went back home.

Later that evening one of their family members was looking for me. When he saw me, he shouted with joy, shouting that his nephew was alive! He was drinking milk and was recovering. Praise God! The baby boy was totally healed. He is now grown and healthy.

By believing and trusting what Jesus has promised we can see miracles happen. Many times we only believe in part and hope in part, and our mouth speaks with something other than faith. Proverbs 18:21 says, "Death and life are in the power of the tongue." Many people speak the wrong things about themselves—the speak death instead of life.

The first thing I want you to know is that the enemy puts wrong thoughts in our minds. Satan is the father of lies (John 8:44). When he lies to us about the pain in our physical body or our situation, it is easy to agree with him. But when we agree with him, what we agree with begins to be spoken. And once we speak it, we are then allowing ourselves to agree with the lies of the enemy. When we say we don't feel good, or we feel sick, the more we speak that over us the more fear will enter, and the more we will see the symptoms manifest in our physical body. We begin to believe it and then say it. Then we begin to feel even sicker. That is why it is very important to dismantle all the wrong things—all the lies which the enemy has sown.

Thousands Of Mosquitoes

Some time ago I began to pray during the early morning hours on the side of the road in a small town. All the stores were closed and I was sitting on their steps near the main road. After a few minutes of trying to pray, I could not continue because thousands of mosquitoes began to bite me. I was constantly scratching myself and thought I needed to quickly finish praying and return to sleep. As I was about to get up from the steps, something leapt in my spirit. I felt as if someone was telling me that I was the temple of God. When I sensed this, my inner man thought and imagined that I was the temple of the Holy Spirit. I suddenly became upset with the mosquitoes and began to talk to them. I told them, "How dare you try to touch me! I am the temple of God and God lives in me! I belong to Jesus. So I bind you in the name of Jesus—you cannot touch me!" Then I began to see myself as God's own temple (God's house). I began to praise God and tell Jesus, "Thank You for making me Your temple." Within no time at all, the mosquitoes could not touch me. They were flying everywhere around me but they could not touch me.

The Scriptures state that we are the temple of God: "Know ye not that ye are the temple of God, and that the Spirit of God dwelleth in you?" (1 Corinthians 3.16). It would do well if we realized how powerful these Scriptures are. Generally speaking, if you are in your own house and if any thieves try to break in and steal from you, you most likely won't be happy and you'll try to stop them. You do not want anyone to break into your house. So if we are the temple of God, why do we allow the devil to harm our body?

Why do we allow the thief in to steal the things purchased for us through Christ?

You need to be aware of the promises of God made unto you. If the promise is for you when you read the Scriptures, then believe it and agree with it. Speak the promises of God out loud and you'll begin to see it; you will see the power of God released as well as His protection over you.

Speaking To The Tree

I was praying in my village, walking up and down the streets in the night hours, looking at the stars and moon as I was worshipping God. Suddenly a thought about Mark 11:23-24 came into my mind. I then began to look towards the trees, which were growing next to the fields. There were many trees there, but I chose one of them, which was much taller than the other ones. I stood in front of that one tree and began to speak to it. I demanded that the tree be removed. I quoted Mark 11:23-24 in my prayer: "Lord, You said in Your Word, when I speak to the mountain, Be thou removed and be thou cast into the sea, without doubting, but believing, it will happen. So, I believe Your Scripture and I am speaking to this tree to be removed." Because there were no oceans or rivers in that village, I only told it to be removed from that place. Then I continued to walk up and down the roads, praising God.

In my heart I believed God heard my prayers. I saw in my spirit that the tree was removed. I kept praising God as I walked back and forth. Every time I would come close to the tree, I would close my eyes and imagine the tree gone. I continued to do this for a long time before going back to sleep.

In the early morning I received a call from another town, inviting me to go there for three days. I had totally forgotten about praying for the tree to be gone. After three days I was on my way home, and when I came closer to the place where I had prayed, it felt as though somebody was holding my neck and turning it towards that place. Suddenly I turned back to where the tree was, and was shocked to see the place empty! The exact three I had commanded was now gone! His Word has power! It still moves mountains and uproots the trees of our problems. It is nothing other than the power of Jesus.

The Dry Thornbush

God often visits me in different ways. On the road of a particular town, I would always notice there was a huge, thorny bush that was overgrown and withered. Every time I saw it, it concerned me. The children would often pass close to it and I thought that maybe someone would get hurt on it someday. When I saw it, I would think that somehow it needed to be removed, even though it had been there for almost two years.

Then one day I began to be very irritated. I asked myself why I had not already prayed against it and commanded it to be removed. "This time I won't command the bush to go away," I thought to myself. "Instead, I want the bush to be burned up." I spoke to it: "Let this bush be burned away in Jesus' name!" I was shocked because within a week's time it was completely burned up. When I questioned myself about why I hadn't done this earlier, I sensed that God will always honor our faith in Him. Everything is possible to the one who believes.

But at the same time we cannot use God's Word for sinful things. He is not the Author of confusion, but is the Prince of Peace.

The Dog Who Barked

One day I took a mile-long walk after my prayers to visit some of my friends. There are many street dogs in India, and as I was walking through the town I was thinking about something when a dog approached me, barking very loudly. He came so close that I jumped from where I was walking because it scared me. I felt very upset and began to complain in my mind, "Lord how could this happen, I am Your child. How can You allow the dogs to scare me like this?" I began to confess that I am a child of God and I solely belong to Him. I began to bind fear and remembered when God sent angels to protect Daniel when he was thrown into the lion's den. And then prayed, "Please send Your angels to protect me."

After meeting my friends I was walking back home on the same road as when I met the stray dog. When I came to the place, the same dog ran up to me, barking loudly, even closer than before! When I saw the dog, I bound the dog in Jesus' name. As I did this, the dog could no longer bark at all. It began to make a strange sound as if someone were choking the neck of the dog. Then it made a big noise as if someone were hitting it. And then the dog ran off. And I was free to pass on that road without being pestered by this dog.

Healing And Miracles

I saw in my spirit the very things I would spoke and believed. I kept praising God for what I saw. It was only then that I began to see mighty things happen because Jesus said that we could speak to the mountain without doubt, being full of faith, and what we spoke would happen. And Proverbs says that life and death are in the power of our tongues. In the Old Testament, Abraham, Isaac, and Jacob spoke the blessings over their families and specific situations, and they all came to pass. God had given them power to speak blessings with their words and what they actually spoke would happen. There is power in our words when they are mixed with faith.

Miracles and signs are going to explode when we begin to speak from our mouth what we see in our spirit and believe in our heart. I practiced this according to what the Bible said, and my circumstances began to change. It has been very important to seeing God's hand in my life and a change in my circumstances. We must say exactly what the Bible says about us, standing in the authority which God has given to us.

In India, many years back, people used to play songs and music very loudly so that the people attending festivals or functions couldn't really rest. Sometimes when I would walk and pray, that loud music would distract my attention and I wouldn't be able to focus on prayer, so I would speak out against them. I would see in my spirit that in no time at all, they would be stopped and peace would return. And other times when I would be traveling by bus to go to certain places and the bus wouldn't have a stop there, I would pray and believe the bus would stop wherever I needed it to. Then the bus would stop and I would be able to get off exactly where I wanted to. I would practice in the small things before eventually beginning to do it for healings and miracles.

A Boy's Stomach Crushed

During the time of learning and practicing my faith, I was in a place called Hubli. I had a young friend who was eleven or twelve years old come to me crying and shaking. He and another friend were bicycling in the street as a tractor came and collided against his friend, injuring his stomach. His friend was completely bruised and crushed so bad that they could do nothing for him medically. As he was in Intensive Care fighting for his life, I was allowed with special permission into the Intensive Care room. I began to speak and pray that God would re-create and heal his stomach. I bound the spirit of death in the name of Jesus and released the life of Jesus into him.

After I was done I came out of the Intensive Care room and met his crying parents, telling them not to be worried because God was going to raise their son. The doctors had already given up on his life. They said he would not make it for another night. He did make it through the night and so the doctor told them that they could do nothing else for the boy. They had already operated and they weren't able to do anything else. So they transferred him to another hospital where he became very serious. My friend told me this, so I went away to pray for this child. The other hospital had found out during his x-rays that the first hospital had left some of the operating instruments inside of him, such as scissors, thinking the boy was going to be dead soon. The second hospital removed everything left by the first and fixed him. After I had prayed and left, I went back to my place and did not hear about this little boy again for some time.

But exactly after a year and a half, I was standing with a little boy who brought me to pray with him and was having a chat. I saw from afar a boy bicycling towards me with a smile, waving his hand. The boy on the bicycle asked me if I remembered him. I told him I didn't remember who he was. It turned out it was the same boy who was dying in the hospital from the accident and God has completely healed him!

The Boy Born Blind

Once I understood the power my words contained, what speaking and believing accomplished, I started using them for the Kingdom of God. At the same time, God blessed me with a healing anointing and I began to use that also to preach to and pray for the sick. When I began praying for the sick, I started seeing mighty things happen. I saw the deaf healed, even some people who were born deaf and blind received their hearing and sight. Others who had tumors and cancer were healed.

One time I was in Naregal preaching in the open air and praying for the sick. People started to get healed and testified of what God was healing them of. There was a boy around eight years old who jumped on the stage and came to me. He said he was blind and that he was able to see now! When I looked into his eyes, there were no retina, no eyeballs; they looked like crooked flesh instead of where the eyes should be. But he said that he could see me. I put my hand up, showed him my fingers, and asked him if he could touch my hand and if he could tell me how many fingers I had up. He kept saying everything correctly. He was able to touch my hand because he was perfectly seeing everything. It really blew my mind what God had done! When he finished testifying, he ran off the stage, jumped in the crowd, and began to tell everyone what God had done for him. The people were so shocked because they knew this boy had been blind. Everywhere I went I saw these types of miracles happen. People were really blessed by the power of God, which was demonstrated so visibly.

Brain Damage Is Healed

A few years ago I was in a town preaching in an open air healing crusade. There was a tremendous anointing for healing that was present—many of the people there were being healed. I noticed on the first day of the evening meeting that there were a few people holding a young boy around sixteen years old. He was hanging off the chair and couldn't sit properly. He looked as if he was falling out of the chair but wasn't because people were supporting him and holding him up.

I usually pray a general prayer for everyone present who is sick without laying hands on them, but the Spirit of God told me to go and lay hands upon this young boy who was struggling to sit in the chair. As I got closer to him, I saw his tongue was hanging out of his mouth (he could not speak) and saliva was coming out too. He looked like he was in a terrible and serious condition. I found out that somebody had hit this young boy on the head with a sharp, metal rod, which ended up damaging his brain. He medically became a vegetable. The doctor refused to keep him in the hospital because he was going to die. Their family brought him back home without any hope and extremely disappointed. But some of his good friends, when they saw that there was a healing meeting in their town, persuaded their parents to bring this boy to my meeting. I laid hands on him and prayed for him as I felt the anointing flowing through me. When finished, I went back to the stage and continued the meeting for the night.

On the second day I was again prompted by the Holy Spirit to go and lay hands on this particular boy. I obeyed and did so. Then on the third day, the last day of my meeting, when I was taking the testimonies, I was so amazed as this young boy, who couldn't walk, talk, or think, came upon the stage! He was walking and testified that he was completely healed! This miracle shook the whole town!

The following year that village invited me for another open air healing crusade. There was a small park there with many trees, where I went and sat to pray, where no one could see me. As I was praying I suddenly heard a few people walking towards me. So I began to wonder to myself,

"Who are these people that are coming towards me while I'm praying?" There was a bunch of young boys who were coming to meet with me. I was hesitant to talk to them because I was in the middle of praying. But the boys said they needed to tell me something. They pushed one of the young boys to the front and said to me, "Do you remember this boy?" The boy looked handsome, strong, and healthy—lots of hair and smiling. I responded, "I don't remember you." The boy said, "I was the person who was dying one year ago. My brain was damaged. God healed me completely." I could not believe my eyes! It was such a powerful miracle that took place! He looked very different from when I saw him last. But when God does something, He does it perfectly.

Mighty Healings (HDkota)

When I went to HDkota near Mysore, India, there was a three-day conference for a poor village with a few hundred people in attendance. Since I traveled from a very far village I was physically worn out. I was very tired and didn't want to preach or teach that day. So I shared for a few minutes and then began to pray for the sick. After I prayed, I asked if anyone received healing in their body. Many hands immediately shot up in the air. I thought the people in this village misunderstood me, so I slowly explained: "Only those of you who were physically healed should raise their hands." The same amount of hands went up again. I then told a few pastors and leaders to check them thoroughly and then send them up on stage to testify of what God had done.

The first woman to come up and testify really touched me. She said she came to the meeting with a tumor in her stomach the size of a football and now it had completely vanished! Another woman approached the stage and said she had a goiter in her throat which dissolved. All of my physical fatigue left me as I heard these testimonies. A boy came up and said he was deaf and now his ears were opened.

In the mean time I saw a woman near the stage walking with a hunched back. She came up onto the stage and showed her back. She had a massive lump which made her look like she had a hunched back. Half of the original lump had disappeared and half still remained. I told her, "Go back to where you were sitting and do not return until you have seen the complete healing." There were many others that came and testified about their healings and deliverances from demonic possession. When this was done the same hunched back woman returned. But this time her back was straight! She walked straight and there was no sign of a lump on her back. It really amazed me. Praise God for these healings!

When it came close to the end of the meetings, there were a few people who were sitting in the back shouting and screaming. I asked why they were screaming, and they all shouted in unison there was another testimony that needed to be shared. I saw from far away a woman who was very thin, just skin and bones. A couple was with her as she came on the stage and said she was in the last stages of breast cancer—it had spread all over. She had fainted a few times but people still carried her to the meeting. While I was praying, she said it felt like someone was hitting her cancer with a rod. When she felt the place where the cancer was, she could feel it breaking and oozing out of her body. The pain immediately left her and she felt the strength from God and began to walk. Praise God for who He is and what He has done through these miracles!

A Deaf Woman In Germany

I was recently in Germany and I saw a tremendous anointing when I prayed for people. Several people who had arthritis for many years, and even though they had a lot of treatment, and went to different specialists and hospitals, and still nothing happened; but God healed them that night.

A few days later at different meetings in Germany seven deaf people were healed. I was speaking at a Full Gospel Businessmen's meeting when God gave me a word of knowledge about deafness in the ears. When I called out that condition, a woman stood up with a machine hanging out of one of her ears. I asked her whether she could hear or not. She said she couldn't so I called her to the front and had her take out the machine that was hanging in her ears. When she took it out, she jumped in shock and began to exclaim, "I can hear! I can hear! It is too loud!" When I asked her what was wrong with her, she said that when she was around seven or eight years old, she damaged both of her eardrums, which meant she could never again hear normally. With the help of a medical procedure, she could hear very little. Praise God, she got totally healed! Then she counted and said, "Wow! I was deaf for sixty years, but God healed me now!" With tears and joy she began to praise God!

We recently had another meeting in Pittsburgh. There was a powerful witness from the Holy Spirit that God was going to be healing people. Among the ones God healed was a woman deaf in one ear. Her son-in-law had a problem with his kidneys, which got healed as well. There were several others who had arthritis and were healed that day also.

But one of the most amazing miracles that day was this: there was a young woman, who both of her lungs had collapsed, who came to the meeting. She also had MS and many other complications. The doctor had completely given up on her. She could not stand or walk for more than a couple of minutes at a time. In this meeting, God touched her and healed her. Suddenly both of her lungs began to function normally; she could stand and walk for twenty minutes with no problems at all. Her whole family was so amazed at what God had done for her. They were all crying and praising God!

When we learn to rely on God in faith, then we will see mighty things happen.

Chapter 16

Difference Between Faith And Senses

When I understood the difference between the spirit man and the natural man, it was then I that began to see a greater manifestation of the power of God in my life. I began to see more miracles and more healings take place. Sensing with only the natural man brings only natural results. But sensing with the spirit man brings miraculous results.

Many of us make a big mistake when we rely on all of our senses, and not on faith. God can do much greater and more powerful things through faith than He can with all of our senses put together. It's my desire for you to know what you see, what you hear, what you smell, and what you feel, because these senses can bring wrong information that contradicts your belief system. Faith always springs from the heart, from your spirit, not from your natural senses. This is why Paul wrote of all Christians, "We walk by faith, not by sight" (2 Corinthians 5:7).

The Gospel of Matthew tells the story of the time Jesus walked on water in the middle of the night to help His disciples (Matthew 14:22-33). Jesus had sent the disciples into a boat while He went by Himself into a mountain to pray. Throughout the night the boat was in the midst of the sea while Jesus was spending some time in prayer. But in the early morning, being still dark, Jesus saw the boat "in the midst of the sea, tossed with waves" because "the wind was contrary."

Since they were in the middle of the sea and He was on land, then it couldn't have been with His natural sight that He saw them struggling with the wind and waves. I believe He saw them in His spirit and knew they were in trouble. So Jesus walked on the water to help them. When they saw Him coming towards them, they "were troubled" and thought He was a spirit, "and they cried out for fear." They didn't understand He had come to help them. But He told them to not be afraid, but to be of good cheer.

When Peter heard that, he asked Jesus to let him walk on the water to Jesus. Peter told Him that if it was really Him, "bid me to come unto thee on the water." And Jesus told him to come! Peter walked on the water! But as he walked a few steps his senses began to operate and faith died out. He heard the sound of the waves and felt the winds all around him; he saw the situation with his natural senses. He felt the water splashing all around him in the dark. He probably even tasted the water as it would have splashed up in his face. All of these physical senses created fear in him, bringing upon him great doubt. And it was because of this doubt that he began to sink in the water before Jesus grabbed hold of him as he cried out.

Many times we allow our natural senses to work against our miracles. For this reason we need to make it known that faith is purely spiritual and it comes from God and through His Word alone. Belief will spring from our heart, from our spirit man. No matter what kind of negative circumstances come through our minds or through our natural five senses, if we hold onto faith, supported by God's Word, then it will work every time. God longs for us to walk by faith in His promises, not by what we see with our physical senses.

Chapter 17

The Power Of Praise And Worship

Another effective way to overcome attacks on our faith is through the power of praise and worship. It is important to make praise and worship an integral part of our lifestyle. Together, they are mentioned over five hundred times throughout the Bible. We must offer praise and worship to our God, who is our defense, in all the battles we face.

Psalm 89:15-18 proclaims,

> Blessed is the people that know the joyful sound: they shall walk, O LORD, in the light of thy countenance. In thy name shall they rejoice all the day: and in thy righteousness shall they be exalted. For thou art the glory of

their strength: and in thy favour our horn shall be exalted. For the LORD is our defence; and the Holy One of Israel is our king.

And Psalm 149:5-9 says of God's people,

Let the saints be joyful in glory: let them sing aloud upon their beds. Let the high praises of God be in their mouth, and a twoedged sword in their hand; To execute vengeance upon the heathen, and punishments upon the people; To bind their kings with chains, and their nobles with fetters of iron; To execute upon them the judgment written: this honour have all his saints. Praise ye the LORD.

In the Book of Acts we read about the power of praise. Paul and Silas were beaten and placed in prison. What did they do when they were persecuted? They didn't sit around in pity and grumble against God. Acts 16:25 says, "And at midnight Paul and Silas prayed, and sang praises unto God." The result of their prayer and praise was astounding. Luke records, "And suddenly there was a great earthquake, so that the foundations of the prison were shaken: and immediately all the doors were opened, and every one's bands were loosed" (Acts 16:26). The praise of Paul and Silas broke the chains of all the prisoners. And eventually the jailer was even saved. Praise contains the power to break bondages.

When King Jehoshaphat heard that three kings were coming against him, he became very scared and worried. He went before God and cried unto Him. The Lord told him to take the people who were able to worship, put them in the front of the army, and let them worship and play music as they entered the battlefield. God would fight for them. When King Jehoshaphat obeyed the command of God, we read how God fought for them and defeated all of their enemies.

God told Joshua and all the people of Israel to march around the walls of Jericho for six days. Then on the seventh day, God asked them to circle the city seven times. On the seventh time the priests were to blow the trumpets and the rest of the congregation was to shout at the top of their lungs. When they did according to the word of the Lord, the walls came down and the Israelites defeated the city of Jericho. They had victory over the enemy because they praised and worshipped God (Joshua 6).

When Jonah was in the whale's belly, he repented and began to praise the God of Heaven. The whale could no longer hold him when the praises began to come out of his mouth. The whale vomited him out of its mouth onto dry land. In all of these things we see that praising God with a joyful heart will bring God immediately into your situation, able and willing to help you.

So much of the Bible talks about the importance of praise and worship. The majority of the Psalms are filled with praise and worship, as David and others express their deepest desires to God.

Praise and worship are like incense before the throne of God, as symbolized throughout the Old Testament tabernacle in the time of Moses. It has two parts: the holy place and the holy of holies. In the holy place we see the table of showbread, the candlestick, and the altar of incense. The altar of incense was kept by the entrance to the holy of holies. In order to get there the High Priest would go through the brazen altar, which represents the sacrifice of Jesus, to the laver, representing sanctification through the Word of God. Then he would come to the table of showbread in the holy place, which signifies the fellowship of God's Word. Then he would approach the candlestick, representing the presence of the Holy Spirit and His gifts. It was only then that he would come to the altar of incense, which symbolizes our worship and praise to God. When all of that was completed, the High Priest would then offer incense (praise and worship) before he was allowed to enter the holy of holies, where the Ark of the Covenant was kept, where he would meet with God and talk with Him.

The praise that breaks down the strongholds of the devil is praise made to God with all instruments, with loud shouts, clanging cymbals, with trumpets, stringed instruments, and pianos. But in the act of worship you very gently love and adore Him. In worship we are enabled to talk to Him about how great and loving He is. Worship is not so much talking about Him as it is talking to Him. God dwells among the praises of His people (Psalm 22:3). Many times during real worship, people experience seeing Jesus or angels. Some people have even heard the voices of angels during worship.

Throughout the Bible there is evidence that victory was given by God when praise and worship went before Him. In the Old Testament, Joshua and Jehoshaphat won the battle as they worshipped: that means they captured kingdoms. But Luke tells the story of Jesus being tempted by the devil (Luke 4). The devil showed Him "all the kingdoms of the world in a moment of time" and told Him, "All this power will I give thee, and the glory of them: for that is delivered unto me; and to whomsoever I will I give it. If thou therefore wilt worship me, all shall be thine." Then Jesus commanded him, "Get thee behind me, Satan: for it is written, Thou shalt worship the Lord thy God, and him only shalt thou serve." (Luke 4:5-8).

The devil deceived Adam and took all the authority to the kingdoms, but praise God that Jesus died on the cross of Calvary! He broke Satan's power over the nations and He has taken the keys back! He has given us the authority, power, and dominion to rule over each circumstance and situation, even over the world. If we stand in that authority and dominion that God has given to us, then we can take the nations and the kingdoms of the world back for His glory. Healing, casting out demons, raising the dead, destroying the powers of the enemy in the towns and cities, we can establish the Kingdom of God. God will give us a kingly anointing just like David had. We can also stay in this anointing on a consistent basis if we obey, worship, and praise the Lord.

When the kings of the earth planned against the Lord Himself and His anointed people, God sat in the Heavens and laughed at them (Psalm 2). He then promised in Psalm 2:7-8: "I will declare the decree: the LORD hath said unto me, Thou art my Son; this day have I begotten thee. Ask of me, and I shall give thee the heathen for thine inheritance, and the uttermost parts of the earth for thy possession." God promised Jesus and us that He is giving us the nations as our inheritance. And in Isaiah we see that God promises the nations will come by themselves.

When we learn to praise and worship, we build a very strong presence of God around us. When we have the high praises of God in our mouth as well as the two-edged sword in our hand (the Word of God), then we will bring the vengeance and punishment of God upon the demonic forces. Through the power of the Holy Spirit and the Word of God we can bind principalities, powers, and the rulers of darkness that are over the kingdoms of this world (Psalm 149:6-9). And this kind of power will only come as we give wholeheartedly give ourselves to God in praise and worship.

Chapter 18

The Power Of The Holy Spirit

I n this chapter I would like to talk about the person of the Holy Spirit whom Jesus spoke about in the Gospel of John. Jesus said he was going to send another Comforter, which was the Holy Spirit, after He went away. The Holy Spirit was going to bring comfort to us and share things about Jesus with us. He is the one who was going to lead us and the one who will guide us. He is the one who now resides with us and brings peace to our hearts.

John wrote, "But the anointing which ye received of him abideth in you, and ye need not that any man teach you: but as the same anointing teacheth you of all things, and is truth, and is no lie, and even as it hath taught you, ye shall abide in him" (1 John 2:27). Though we see the Holy Spirit talked much about in the Bible, yet there are certain symbols that seem to represent Him: fire, dove, water, wind, and the breadth of God.

In the Old Testament the Hebrew word for the Holy Spirit is *ruwach*, meaning wind or breath of God. When we see all of these symbolic references we often forget that the Holy Spirit is a person, God Himself. In Joel 2:28 and Acts 2:17 we see the promise of God: "And it shall come to pass in the last days, saith God, I will pour out of my Spirit upon all flesh." This is an amazing promise to everyone who hears it. God promised that He is going to give His Spirit to *all*. That means you are also one of these He promised to pour out His Spirit on.

So when we receive the baptism of the Holy Spirit according to Acts 1:8—"But ye shall receive power, after that the Holy Ghost has come upon you"—then we receive the power of God. The power used here in Greek is the word *dunamis*. This means dynamite! When the Holy Spirit comes upon us we will become like dynamite to the kingdom of Satan. Jesus also promised us: "Behold, I have given you authority to tread on serpents and scorpions, and over all the power of the enemy, and nothing will injure you" (Luke 10:19. NASB).

When we talk about the Holy Spirit and the power we receive from above, we should also know who we are and how God created us to function. This will really help us stand in the right place with the authority of God to see the mighty things He promised us come to be.

In the beginning we saw how God made us—He created us in His own image. When God was creating the universe, when He was creating the heavens and the earth, the moon and the stars, including the human beings, He was a Spirit. Jesus confirms this for us in John's Gospel: "God is a Spirit: and they that worship him must worship him in spirit and in truth" (4:24).

Though we were initially created in His own image, as a spirit being, part of God Himself, we see that sin destroyed the relationship between God and man. Our spirit man was dead until we encountered Jesus, receiving God's forgiveness for all our sins which we committed (1 John 1:8) and washed through the blood of Jesus. After receiving Him as our personal Savior, our spirit man is born again (John 3:3). We receive new life through Jesus. However, it was not finished at the point we received forgiveness of sins, but we needed to be filled with the Holy Spirit. The Holy Spirit is the one who convicted us of our sin and helped us to be born again into His Kingdom. He is also the one who sealed us as His children. The same Holy Spirit is going to come upon us in a different ways as God promised in Joel 2:28.

The Holy Spirit being poured upon us is called the baptism in the Holy Spirit. We are immersed in the Holy Spirit or filled with the Spirit. The He brings nine gifts as well as nine fruits that are meant to operate in our lives. It is our responsibility to develop the nine fruits and the nine gifts of the Holy Spirit.

I'm going to explain to you what kind of ability God gives us in our inner man to make the impossible things possible. The things which we cannot physically and mentally do, we can do certain of those things through the Spirit of God. All the new things begin to happen after the Holy Ghost comes upon us. Paul wrote to the Corinthians: "But he who unites himself with the Lord is one with him in spirit" (1 Corinthians 6:17). Our spirit together with God's Spirit can break the boundaries and break the limitations around us. We can do more things beyond our ability by joining with the Holy Spirit.

The Bible speaks about the event which took place two thousand years ago in Jerusalem. When one hundred and twenty people were waiting in the Upper Room, waiting for the promise of Jesus to be fulfilled, on the day of Pentecost the Holy Spirit came like a rushing, mighty wind upon the people. All of them began to speak in tongues as the Holy Spirit gave them utterance. It was a great noise.

Many people who rushed towards the place began to inquire with others, asking about what was going on. There were different nationalities who understood the messages that were being spoken by His disciples as they were declaring the praises of God in other tongues. Some people began to say, "How could this happen because these people don't know the language? How can they speak the languages of different nationalities?" Some people began to say that these people were just drunk.

"But Peter, standing up with the eleven, lifted up his voice, and said unto them, Ye men of Judaea, and all ye that dwell at Jerusalem, be this known unto you, and hearken to my words: For these are not drunken, as ye suppose, seeing it is but the third hour of the day" (Acts 2:14-15). When this experience took place, the gospel began to spread rapidly, followed by signs, wonders, and miracles.

The same experience is given to every person who believes today if they are hungry for it. It is very important to have this experience with the Holy Spirit for the empowerment of our lives. After we are baptized in the Holy Spirit, we also see one of the gifts in operation, which is the gift of speaking in tongues. God specifically designs this particular gift, among the eight other gifts, for us to use all the time so that we can be connected with God the Father Himself. We are going to learn how this particular gift is going to help us to be tapped into the Kingdom of Heaven.

Chapter 19

Are You Thirsty?

God gives to every man the gifts of His Spirit according to His will (1 Corinthians 12:4, 7-11). From the parable of the talents we see that God gives to each man according to that individual's ability to receive from the Lord (Matthew 25:14-30). To some He may give one gift, some may receive two, while others may receive five. But everyone gets the gifts according to the will of God. One thing is certain, however, that God gives to *every* individual, though the measure He gives may vary from person to person.

Paul wrote, "Blessed be the God and Father of our Lord Jesus Christ, who hath blessed us with all spiritual blessings in heavenly places in Christ" (Ephesians 1:3). God has already blessed us with every gift and every blessing we will possibly need in life. It is all stored in our inner man when we are baptized in the Holy Spirit. The gifts manifest according to the need of the people as well our faithfulness to God, our ability, and our desire. That's why Paul tells Timothy to stir up the gifts of the Holy Spirit that reside within him (2 Timothy 1:6). But most of all, they all work together according to His will.

Our God gives a measure to everyone (Matthew 25:15, 1 Corinthians 12:7)—He wants to anoint every person. However, I would like to ask you: are you ready to receive what He wants to give you? Are you willing to let Him anoint you? Are you thirsty enough to drink the living water He provides? Jesus said, "If any man thirst, let him come unto me, and drink," inviting everyone to receive the Holy Spirit. He then continued, "He that believeth on me, as the scripture hath said, out of his belly shall flow rivers of living water" (John 7:37-38). Are you thirsty?

We are controlled by what we are filled with. If a person is drunk or filled with wine, then the wine controls them. And we all know what harm is caused by this. This is why Ephesians 5:18 admonishes us, "And be not drunk with wine, wherein is excess; but be filled with the Spirit." We are to be filled with and controlled by the Spirit of God.

Imagine the state of a person who is completely and utterly filled with the Spirit of God. Such a person is controlled and influenced by the Holy Spirit in all they do and all they say. The Holy Spirit directs every move of that person. Jesus was a perfect example. He only did what He saw His Father do and only said what He heard His Father say. We can only realize the difference a Spirit-filled person can make in this world when they are filled with His Spirit.

So when the Bible says that a person was "filled" with the Holy Spirit, it doesn't mean they were only filled up half way, but they were completely filled, overflowing with His presence and power. The Book of Acts abounds with examples of people who were filled with the Holy Spirit. No wonder they could make such a huge impact on the world.

Just as it is possible for those addicted to alcohol to be immersed in it day after day, and for it to control their lives, so in the same way it is also possible for born-again Christians to be immersed in the Holy Spirit day in and day out, letting Him guide us and control us. If a born-again Christian will be immersed in the Holy Spirit every minute of the day, then there will be no chance for sin to enter their life.

You only drink as much as you want. Imagine you are invited to a party where juice is served with an instruction that everyone can drink as much juice as they want. Most of the people at the party will drink a few glasses, but some will want to drink as much as they can because they are thirsty and they know that there is plenty of juice available. In God's Kingdom, everyone who is thirsty is to come and drink of the living water He provides. You can drink as much as you want of that living water. But how thirsty are you?

Is your thirst for carnal things? Then that thirst must be replaced by the thirst for living water. You can be filled as much as you are thirsty for. If you are thirsty for God and His Spirit, God will fill you to overflowing. You can see the difference you can make as He fills you. This is a promise of Jesus: "In the last day, that great day of the feast, Jesus stood and cried, saying, If any man thirst, let him come unto me, and drink. He that believeth on me, as the scripture hath said, out of his belly shall flow rivers of living water" (John 7:37-38).

Many Christians experience only a few drops of living water and become very satisfied. They are content with what they have received. However, God wants to give us much more than we can ask or even imagine.

How I was Baptized by the Holy Spirit

I went to a meeting with my friend many years ago and saw many young people speaking in tongues. I began to inquire about how this could happen to them. I talked to many pastors and many men of God about what I saw. Everyone explained why we should receive the baptism of the Holy Spirit and the gift of speaking in tongues. From that time on, I began to ask God to give me this gift as well. I also prayed for the Holy Spirit to anoint me.

I kept praying for almost an entire year to receive this experience of the Holy Spirit before anything happened. I went to several meetings at many different churches, asking different men of God to pray for me to be filled with the Holy Spirit. Nothing happened. This caused me to be even more desperate to be filled. In some of those meetings I saw people who were filled with the Holy Spirit and they couldn't stand—they were falling down under the power of God. Some of them were rolling around on the ground after being filled by His Spirit. I was so desperate. I thought that if I fell down and rolled like them that I would be filled with the Holy Spirit, but nothing happened when I tried that. I knew that if I were filled with the Holy Spirit, I would be a different person.

When my final exam came in college, I was sharing a hostel room in the city of Hubli with a friend of mine, John. We were both studying a lot for our exams. One particular day I was tired and told my friends that I wanted to sleep for a couple of hours, and asked them to wake me up at three in the morning. Before I went to sleep, however, I opened the Bible and the Scripture came alive in Romans 16:20: "And the God of peace shall bruise Satan under your feet shortly. The grace of our Lord Jesus Christ be with you. Amen." I immediately underlined this Scripture and then fell asleep.

While sleeping I had a dream. I saw an ugly tree growing in my room. There was a spider web and spiders on the tree along with a big black snake. I tried to kill the snake with a small sword. Somebody asked me, "How are you going to kill it?" I said, "It is easy. I can kill it in the name of Jesus." Then I went and killed that snake in Jesus' name. Right then my friend woke me up from my dream. It was three o'clock and my friend was going to bed to get some sleep. As he went and laid down on his bed, within a minute he began to make some sounds just like someone was choking him. So I called his name aloud, asking him what was happening. John struggled to wake up and told me that he saw a demon come and sit on his chest, choking him. I was so scared when he told me that because I had never heard of such things in my life.

Even though I didn't want to say it, I told him to rededicate his life to Jesus and ask God to forgive him. He was a backslidden believer. We both knelt down and began to pray together. While he was recommitting his life to Jesus, I also asked God to make me whole and holy by cleansing me through His blood. While I was still praying, the Holy Spirit suddenly descended upon me. I commanded the devil to go away in the name of Jesus with a very loud voice, but it was not me who was speaking, rather the Spirit of God speaking through me. I never prayed that kind of prayer in my life. I never saw anyone casting out demons before. But I was praying with such power, authority, and boldness.

I was surprised as the Holy Spirit continued to fall on me. I did not know how to continue to have this experience, so I just stopped right there. My roommate, John, was completely delivered from the demonic oppression and he gave his life to Jesus. Praise God for his deliverance as well as his rededication to Christ! I went in the early morning to my friend's house and told everyone what had happened. Everyone knew it was the Holy Spirit that had come upon me. It was such a joy to me and a very powerful, life-changing experience.

Empowered By The Holy Spirit

I controlled myself after that for a few days, not allowing the gift of tongues to flow through my mouth. My friends, who were already filled with the Spirit, took me away from the town and went into the fields to spend some time in prayer.

There was about ten of us that night, at about eleven o'clock. They told me when the Holy Spirit falls upon me not to control my tongue, but to speak whatever the Holy Spirit gives me to say. I was waiting in anticipation. We were all standing in a circle, holding hands. We began to sing the Hallelujah chorus, which is very common all over the world, and when we came to the second line, the Holy Spirit began to fall on me. I could not sing more than three or four more words—He hit me very powerfully. I fell on the black soil, beginning to speak in tongues very loudly, and singing in the spirit. As I was down on the ground it began to rain. But I was so caught up in God's presence that I didn't care what was going on around me. I just kept going and experiencing the presence of God in a fresh way. It was such ecstasy and delight.

Then my friends began to stop me and tried to wake me out of my experience with God. I wondered why they were stopping me. After they managed to stop me and get my attention, I was thinking that only a few minutes had passed. But they said it was already the morning, the sun was rising! I had no idea I had been speaking in tongues since eleven o'clock the night before!

Needless to say that my life was completely changed from that point on. When I got back to my room, my throat was soar from speaking all night. I needed to sleep for a couple of hours, but at the same time I was worried that if I stopped speaking in tongues I might lose the gift. So I would just sleep for a few minutes, then get up and speak in tongues for a little bit. I would be filled with joy and then I would lie back down and fall asleep again. I repeated this for an entire day. Even though I was physically tired at night, I enjoyed my routine of sleeping for a bit and then praying in the spirit.

I would continue to speak in tongues while standing on the bus to and from college. I would speak in tongues everywhere I walked. My non-Christian friends would take notice that my mouth never stopped moving, even though they couldn't hear what I was saying. They asked why I was constantly talking. And of course it was difficult for me to explain to them because I myself did not know much about it. I still gave them some answers though.

So after a few weeks I was charged up by the Holy Spirit and began to have dreams and visions. Then later on the gifts of the Spirit began to operate in my life. It all happened within a month or two after I was baptized in the Holy Spirit. God would show me specific details about certain people's lives. And then when I would talk to them, they would sometimes be shocked and some would even become scared because there was no possible way I could have known those things about them. They wondered how I knew about their life. I didn't know those were the gifts of the Holy Spirit at the time.

It was during this time I began to study 1 Corinthians 14:2 and 4.

> For he that speaketh in an unknown tongue speaketh not unto men, but unto God: for no man understandeth him; howbeit in the spirit he speaketh mysteries...He that speaketh in an unknown tongue edifieth himself; but he that prophesieth edifieth the church.

We are edified and become stronger in the Lord as we pray in the spirit. I was surprised as I understood how true the Bible was. Every time I spoke in tongues, I was charged by the power of God as well as my physical strength was renewed. My mind was filled with God's peace and I experienced the joy of the Lord in its fullness. I really praise God for all the experiences He has given me. It has been many years since being filled with the Spirit, but I still daily practice praying in the spirit. It is one of the most important things I do in my day.

CHAPTER 20

The Language That Unlocks The Heavenly Realm

The Gift Of Speaking In Tongues

When the Holy Spirit descended for the first time as one hundred and twenty people gathered in the upper room, the people began to speak in tongues (Acts 2:1-4). As Peter was at Cornelius' house, the Holy Spirit began to fall upon the people in the middle of his preaching, and they began to speak in tongues as well (Acts 10:44-46). And in Ephesus Paul laid hands upon the disciples and the Holy Ghost descended on them and they began speaking in tongues and prophesying (Acts 19:6). Speaking in tongues is a gift that is evident throughout the New Testament.

Paul explains for us some of the experiences that took place in Acts (1 Corinthians 14). The Bible explains differing kinds of tongues: there's known tongues and unknown tongues, tongues of angels and heavenly tongues. And there is also the various languages or tongues heard around the world, differing in sounds and dialects. But, make no mistake about it, there is a language from God which will be given to us when the Holy Spirit comes upon us. I want to share with you some important insights about praying in the spirit, or speaking in tongues.

Personal Edification

The first benefit of praying in tongues is that our spirits are edified. Paul writes, "For he that speaketh in an unknown tongue speaketh not unto men, but unto God: for no man understandeth him; howbeit in the spirit he speaketh mysteries" (1 Corinthians 14:2). Paul is teaching us that when we speak in tongues we are directly speaking to God. When we're speaking in the heavenly language, no one will be able to understand what we are saying or what we are praying for. We will be speaking "mysteries." So it looks strange and absurd to human thinking, but it does not matter what the natural man thinks. God made a way for us to stay connected to Him by speaking in unknown tongues. Continually utilizing this gift will help us to live strong, successful lives.

Then Paul reiterates himself: "He that speaketh in an unknown tongue edifieth himself" (1 Corinthians 14:4). The more we speak in tongues, the more edified we become. This is why Paul could confidently say, "I thank my God, I speak with tongues more than ye all" (1 Corinthians 14:18). He knew what would happen if one prayed in the spirit; that is why he constantly spoke in tongues and received the benefits thereof.

Paul wrote more books of the Bible than any other author because he received more revelation from Heaven. The more we speak in tongues, the more edified we will become and the more we will speak mysteries in the spirit. Because of this we will be receiving many revelations. When we are speaking in tongues, no one will understand what we're saying, including the demonic powers. It is one-to-one conversation between us and God.

There are varieties of the gift of tongues. In 1 Corinthians 12:10 it says, "To another the working of miracles; to another prophecy; to another discerning of spirits; to another divers kinds of tongues; to another the interpretation of tongues." Different things will happen as we speak in tongues. He will put that gifting within us, using us bring blessing to us and those around us. And all of this will be according to the will of God.

The following is a list of twenty attributes of speaking in tongues. When we speak in tongues:

1. We will be speaking to God, not to anyone else—"For he that speaketh in an unknown tongues speaketh not unto men, but unto God" (1 Corinthians 14:2).
2. No one will understand what we're saying, including both ourselves and the devil—"For no man understandeth him" (1 Corinthians 14:2).
3. We will be speaking mysteries directly to God—"howbeit in the spirit he speaketh mysteries" (1 Corinthians 14:2).
4. We will become very strong and charged by the Holy Spirit as we pray in tongues. Not only that, but we will also be filled with knowledge and understanding, receiving many revelations from Heaven—"He that speaketh in an unknown tongue edifieth himself" (1 Corinthians 14:4).
5. Our spirit is active with the Spirit of God and also deeply connected to God. We will be praying in

the spirit through our spirit—"For if I pray in an unknown tongues, my spirit prayeth" (1 Corinthians 14:14).

6. The Holy Spirit will surpass our natural mind, which is filled with a lot of reasoning, doubt, fear, and limitations. He surpasses all of those things as we give ourself to praying in tongues. He will connect our spirit to His Spirit. By doing that, we will directly receive all the blessings, healings, and revelations that couldn't be received through our natural mind—"but my understanding is unfruitful" (1 Corinthians 14:14).

7. We will be praying in the spirit—"I will pray with the spirit" (1 Corinthians 14:15).

8. God will give us the understanding of what we are praying for in the spirit. Simultaneously we will be praying with our understanding also—"and I will pray with the understanding also" (1 Corinthians 14:15).

9. God will cause us to sing with the spirit (or sing in tongues). He will give His own tune and a song in our heart—"I will sing with the spirit" (1 Corinthians 14:15).

10. When the Holy Spirit gives us a song in the spirit, He will also give us the understanding of the song we are singing along with it—"and I will sing with the understanding also" (1 Corinthians 14:15).

11. When we are praying in the spirit (or speaking in tongues), we will also be blessing God—"Else when thou shalt bless with the spirit" (1 Corinthians 14:16).

12. We will also be praising and thanking God—"at thy giving of thanks" (1 Corinthians 14:16).

13. Sometimes God will give us a foreign language, which we do not know. If the person who speaks that language hears what we're saying, he will understand it. This is what took place in Acts 2, where the people in the upper room spoke in tongues as the Holy Spirit descended. When the people from many nations heard it, they understood what they were saying and were shocked. It was a sign for them—"Wherefore tongues are for a sign, not to them that believe, but to them that believe not" (1 Corinthians 14:22).

14. God knows our physical limitations and spiritual conditions, as well as everything we are going through. He will deal with us when we engage ourself and pray in the spirit, breaking those limitations—"Likewise

the Spirit also helpeth our infirmities" (Romans 8:26).

15. Many times we are limited and don't know what the root cause of our problems are. And since we don't know how to pray for what is really causing our problems, the Holy Spirit will help us come out of our problems as we pray in the spirit—"for we know not what we should pray for as we ought: but the Spirit itself maketh intercession for us with groanings which cannot be uttered" (Romans 8:26).

16. The Holy Spirit is the one who searches the hearts of men and women all over the world, who are in the body of Christ. He knows what the plan of God is for every person. He also knows what they are going through. He will deal with them and help them as we speak in tongues—"And he that searcheth the hearts knoweth what is the mind of the Spirit" (Romans 8:27).

17. The Holy Spirit knows what is best for everyone and what His will is for their lives. When we pray in tongues (pray in the spirit), we will be interceding for the saints all over the world in accordance with the will of God; meeting their needs and setting up protection

for them—"Because he maketh intercession for the saints according to the will of God" (Romans 8:27).

18. God promised to speak to the people through stammering lips and another tongue. Every time we speak in tongues, Isaiah's prophecy is being fulfilled— "For with stammering lips and another tongues will he speak to this people" (Isaiah 28:11).
19. God will bring such a peace and rest that passes all our understanding. Though we are weary, tired, and confused, God will bring rest and peace to our soul— "To whom he said, This is the rest wherewith ye mat cause the weary to rest" (Isaiah 28:12).
20. Not only peace, but God also will bring such a refreshing to us, combined with joy! He will renew our strength like that of the eagle (Isaiah 40:31)— "and this is the refreshing: yet they would not hear" (Isaiah 28:12).

Separation Of The Natural Mind And Inner Man

"For if I pray in an unknown tongue, my spirit prayeth, but my understanding is unfruitful" (1 Corinthians 14:14).

Paul informs us of what will happen as we pray in the spirit. God's Spirit and our spirit will become one as we are baptized in the Holy Spirit. After we experience this life-changing baptism, we are no longer alone—we have the presence and power of God living within us. In fact, God Himself is living within us. He will be our strength, our guide, our teacher, and our protector. He even knows our future.

So this gift of speaking in tongues will help us surpass our natural mind, which is often filled with limitations, fear, doubt, and wrong thoughts. The remedy Paul gives us for this is to pray in the spirit. He says the mind is going to be unfruitful as we pray—this means our spirit man surpasses our natural mind as we directly connect with the Father. The Heavenly Father knows our natural mind is filled with doubt and limitations. So as we continue to do this, our mind will shut down, and the Holy Spirit will help our spirit receive what the Father has for us.

If we pray according to the will of God, then we will receive everything God has for us—all of our needs and our desires will be met. Since our spirit man is created after the image of God, then we need to be led by the Spirit of God (Romans 8:14). Our natural mind is wayward and still contains much of our old nature. This is why the Holy Spirit makes a distinction between our inner man and our natural mind. Otherwise the mind can try to pull us back into reason every time.

The Holy Spirit often uses His Word to help us make that distinction as well: "For the word of God is quick, and powerful, and sharper than any twoedged sword, piercing even to the dividing asunder of soul and spirit, and of the joints and marrow, and is a discerner of the thoughts and intents of the heart" (Hebrews 4:12). So we can see how the Word of God separates the spirit man and the natural mind. It will also separate the thoughts of our mind, the intentions of our heart, and discern our thoughts. The Word and Spirit of God really do a powerful work within us.

Walk Into Your Future

God has created us in a very unique and incredible way. Every time we connect with the Holy Spirit by praying in the spirit, we are connected with the Heavenly Father and are speaking mysteries to Him. The more we speak in tongues, the more God will be downloaded into our spirit man. Our spirit man will become stronger and stronger, helping us grow in the character of God. Many things we've been struggling with, or all the junk we have been carrying, which is our weaknesses of falling into temptation, anger, lust, and pride, break off as we continually pray in the spirit. Those things will chopped away from our life by the Holy Spirit and by speaking in tongues.

I've heard many testimonies of people who have been struggling with all kinds of problems, even various addictions, who are delivered and their weaknesses are broken. This is done so we will walk in holiness, God's love, and humility. Faith also will increase in us and we will become increasingly sensitive to the Holy Spirit. The eyes of our understanding will be opened and we will begin to pray His will for ourself.

James writes, "Every good gift and every perfect gift is from above, and cometh down from the Father of lights, with whom is no variableness, neither shadow of turning" (1:17). God wants to bless you with every good and perfect gift. Every good thing comes from the Heavenly Father. Jesus said something similar in John 10:10, "I am come that they might have life, and that they might have it more abundantly." And Jeremiah 29:11 says, "For I know the thoughts that I think toward you, saith the LORD, thoughts of peace, and not of evil, to give you an expected end." God has the best future for you and a beautiful destiny already prepared. He has chosen you in Him before the foundation of the world:

"According as he hath chosen us in him before the foundation of the world, that we should be holy and without blame before him in love" (Ephesians 1:4). He saw your future already complete. He sees you holy and without blame. He has already prepared beautiful and glorious things for you to accomplish.

When Joseph had a dream as a teenager, he knew that it was his future and destiny. Through the many obstacles and troubles he faced, his dream was fulfilled and came to pass in his later years. Because of this God-given destiny and the dreams he had, there was a process to go through before getting to fulfill those dreams. He went to the pit, was sold into slavery, was tempted by a woman, and then went to prison; but the dream inside of him became more powerful. And it eventually came to pass.

God revealed to Jeremiah that before he was even born, God had already called him to be a prophet to the nations: "Before I formed thee in the belly, I knew thee; and before thou camest forth out of the womb I sanctified thee, and I ordained thee a prophet unto the nations" (Jeremiah 1:5). God had already called him as a prophet before he was even formed in his mother's womb.

Many of us have had dreams, just like Joseph did. Or sometimes we have visions or someone gives us a prophetic word about our future. Those are all pieces of the puzzle for our future—what God has already seen about us before the foundation of the earth. Part of those pieces can be revealed by dreams, visions, and prophecies. God knows the future and He knows what part each of us will play in it. And one of the ways He helps us to walk into our future is by praying in the spirit.

He has already made us to be something, but our human mind tries to reason against the plan of God. This is why the Holy Spirit will help us go from point A to point Z by praying in the spirit. Since God is the Author of the good, peaceful, prosperous, good health, abundance, and life-giving plan, then the Holy Spirit helps us get to that place. We discover all of these as we begin to pray in the spirit on a continual basis.

Since we have so many limitations in our natural mind, the Holy Spirit helps us overcome those as we pray in the spirit. In Romans 8:26 it says, "Likewise the Spirit also helpeth our infirmities: for we know not what we should pray for as we ought: but the Spirit itself maketh intercession for us with groanings which cannot be uttered." We do not know what to pray for by ourselves, but the Holy Spirit helps us to pray exactly according to the will of God. We have many physical, mental, and even spiritual needs that we don't know how to pray for. As we yield ourselves to the Holy Spirit, who knows our present condition as well as the knowledge of our future, He prays the will of God through us.

When the enemy tries to set up bad situations to enslave us, our wise God knows and He can remove those things out of our way. He can destroy the plan of the enemy and bring us safely to the other side. Jesus told his disciples that He wanted to go to the other side of the lake. While they crossed, He fell asleep in the boat. He said what He meant and knew they would reach the other side. While crossing, however, the storm came against the boat. But Jesus was never bothered and He simply commanded the storm to become calm as the disciples woke Him up.

When the Holy Spirit is connecting us with the Father by speaking in tongues, God is talking to us through the Spirit about the future plans He has for us. He is clearing the path for us. No matter what the enemy tries to put in our path, when we begin to pray in the spirit, God will begin to straighten our path. He is helping us walk into our destiny. He is also revealing the mystery of our future—enabling us to walk in it. He will help us complete and fulfill our destiny with success.

Intercession For Us

The Spirit of God makes intercession for us according to God's will when we don't know what to pray for. Romans 8:26 says, "Likewise the Spirit also helpeth our infirmities: for we know not what we should pray for as we ought: but the Spirit itself maketh intercession for us with groanings which cannot be uttered."

Many times we cannot see the deeper things of God because of the limitations of our mind. Our mind can't clearly see our future or grasp the treasure God has kept for us. They can only be discerned and tapped into by the Spirit of God. First Corinthians 2:9-10 puts it this way: "But as it is written, Eye hath not seen, nor ear heard, neither have entered into the heart of man, the things which God hath prepared for them that love him. But God hath revealed them unto us by his Spirit: for the Spirit searcheth all things, yea, the deep things of God." Our natural eyes and ears can't discern the deep things of God. But those things can be revealed to us and understood through the Spirit of God. We can walk into the blessedness of God by praying in the spirit.

It will be helpful to look at Paul's letter to the Ephesians if we are to understand this in more depth. Paul wrote, "Now unto him that is able to do exceeding abundantly above all that we ask or think, according to the power that worketh in us, Unto him be glory in the church by Christ Jesus throughout all ages, world without end. Amen" (Ephesians 3:20-21). The power is already given to us by the Holy Spirit to receive everything we need. It is more than what we can even think or imagine—it is even more than what we can contain. Only that much blessing can be received by the special power of the Holy Spirit.

The God who created us knows the end from the beginning. Praying in tongues helps us discover God's plan and walk in all He has destined us to do. We will be amazed as we begin to see the glory of God manifested in our life as we connect with the power of the Holy Spirit.

We often don't know what to pray for and are not even aware of our deepest needs in our spirit being, in our physical bodies, or in our minds. However, the Holy Spirit knows. He will help us in our infirmities—sicknesses or any other physical disabilities—and in our limitations. When we pray deeper in the spirit, we begin to understand more and begin to bring healing in our spirit, physical body, and our mind.

After I received the baptism in the Holy Spirit, I didn't know how to use this gift, I didn't know the power that could be utilized. I wasn't aware of all God could do through it. The Holy Spirit began to reveal many secrets to me though. One day I was feeling oppressed and sick. I felt so heavy and sad. So I went for a walk and started to worship God and speak in tongues. About fifteen minutes later all the heaviness left, the pain left, and the sadness left. I was so refreshed as God completely restored me. I've also heard stories from others about how when they had some form of sickness that couldn't be medically cured, their faith increased as they prayed in tongues and they were finally healed.

Many men of God, as well as other people who are filled with the Holy Spirit and speak in tongues, will often pray in the spirit a lot when they find themselves in the midst of trouble they don't know how to get out of. God begins to give them revelation and wisdom in order to help them to come out of the situation they are going through.

I was preaching in a church in Germany a few years ago, teaching them about the Holy Spirit and speaking in tongues. A pastor and his wife came to me and said, "We never heard this kind of deep teaching about the gift of speaking in tongues before. We didn't know this would help us in different ways." Then they told me about their teenage son, who had been on drugs for a long time. They had spent a lot of money trying to help him, but nothing could set him free. They said, "We are going to try and pray in the spirit for many more hours." So both the husband and wife faithfully prayed in the spirit for one month. At the end of one month their son came home after not being there for many days. He began to cry and said that he needed God. His parents led him to Christ and he was totally changed from that point. He is now an evangelist, married, and has a son. God is using him so powerfully.

During worship I shared how powerful it is to speak in tongues as well as to worship when I was teaching in Bellary, India. There were three young boys who had come from the city of Mysore, India. Being really impressed by this teaching, they went back home and locked themselves in a hall for three days, praying in tongues and worshipping God for many hours a day. They then felt like they were to go to a certain village to evangelize. They didn't know what or how to do it, but as the Holy Spirit led them, they shared the gospel and prayed for the sick people. They were amazed to see tumors melting under their hands, blind eyes opening, and the deaf hearing!

Direction In Your Life

Someone related this story to me: Smith Wigglesworth went to pray for a girl who was seriously ill. When he began to pray he noticed that the girl was dead. He was so embarrassed he did not know what to do. Fear began to grip him. He began to hear the negative thoughts within his mind. He did not know what to do but pray in the spirit. So he stood there and prayed for a little while, and then he felt the devil laughing at him. Suddenly God began to fill him with an anointing of power and faith and he was able to cast out the spirit of death in Jesus' name. The girl was raised from the dead!

Many of us do not realize what is going on in us and around us. Even though we fail to notice these things, the Holy Spirit can penetrate right into our problem and create a beautiful atmosphere inside and around us. He will bring us out of our situation as we pray in tongues, as this releases great wisdom from the Heavenly Father. Praying in the spirit will take us in the right direction when we don't know what to decide. This is why it is important to be filled with the Spirit of God as well as with the Word of God. God's Spirit always moves in accordance with His Word. So, in order for us to have success, guidance, and direction in our life, it is vital to keep being filled with the Spirit of God and His Word.

Praying in tongues will also help us understand what the enemy is trying to do against us. When he begins to plan bad things against us, the Holy Spirit will help prevent us from falling into a bad situation. In other words, when you pray in the spirit, He can clear your path so that you can walk successfully with God's protection.

God helps me to pray a lot in the spirit so I will be protected from the enemy, before he can do anything to harm me. Even presently, I have so many obligations that need to be done. But after doing what I need to do, I still have to pray to receive God's wisdom and blessing. I got up to pray and it ended up being half past three in the morning before I finished. Then I went to lie back down in my bed, and the Holy Spirit prompted me to pray again. I did not know why, but I kept praying in tongues and God showed me some of the dangerous situations that the enemy is trying to bring against me. I bound those demonic situations and asked God for protection for myself and for my family. Sure enough, after about an hour, there was a big storm with lightning and thunder, which felt really close. God protected us as I continued to pray and it slowly disappeared. There have been three times in my life where I've had something similar happen.

There was one particular time I had a powerful crusade where it was cloudy but not rainy. It began lightning and thundering really badly. The lightning struck close by and burned a few trees. Then on the second morning of another crusade in India, I was traveling in a small vehicle, called an auto rickshaw, with my friend. Suddenly, out of nowhere, it started raining. You would not believe the series of lightning striking and flashing all around me; only fifteen to twenty feet away from me there was fire on a metal wire as well as on the fence. The fence was burning, which was very close and scary. Before I could see this, God had me pray in the spirit and proclaim His promises of protection, and God protected me.

Another time in India, when I was at my parents' house, I was praying one afternoon and it began raining and lightning. The lightning was so strong that it burned a coconut tree close by the house. I could see the fire burning the tree. I was so worried that day because of this. So I told God that it was so close and extremely dangerous. I was in a way complaining, but I continued to pray in the spirit during the whole evening. I fell asleep and had a night vision. In the vision there were two men of God and they said they were sent to pray for me. When they laid hands upon me, I fell down under the power of God and I was taken up into the heavenly realm and stood before the King of kings. God had ordered two angels to take the blood of Jesus and to pour it on me; being poured from shiny jars. Then God told me, "You are protected under My blood." It was a very powerful experience and I was so comforted by God.

Making Intercession For Others

We know the Holy Spirit can help us individually when we are praying in tongues. He will help us to pray for others more effectively as well. But it is also the Holy Spirit who searches our hearts and knows our minds. Paul writes, "For he that searcheth the hearts knoweth what is the mind of the Spirit, because he maketh intercession for the saints according to the will of God" (Romans 8:27). This means He knows what everybody's needs are—spiritually, physically, and mentally. The Holy Spirit not only helps us, but He also wants to help others as we are praying in the spirit. He knows the problems of others and He knows what situations they are going through. So when we pray in tongues, we will be praying the will of God according to their needs. This is what Paul means when he said, "he maketh intercession for the saints according to the will of God" (Romans 8:27).

The mind of God knows everything, what scholars have called His omniscience. And we also know His will is always good and a blessing. People often ask me to pray for them, especially for their physical or financial needs. I begin to pray with the abilities God has been given me, but when I cannot go any further, I begin to receive help from the Holy Spirit as I pray in tongues. The Holy Spirit reveals to me specific things to pray for and guides my prayers. He helps me pray for the exact needs of others. Sometimes I know what I am praying for and God gives me revelation about the people. Other times I do not know what I'm praying for, but I do know I'm praying God's will for the people.

While in Sweden ministering in different churches, I came back very tired at one thirty in the morning. But God inspired me to pray. I did not know what I was praying for, but I continued to pray in tongues while the anointing increased upon me. I felt as if I was caught up in the Spirit. While praying, I saw a pastor in India and felt as though I was in India next to him. I saw he was totally broken in pieces and his heart was shattered. He was weeping and crying. I walked over and placed my arm around him; suddenly I knew he wanted to kill himself. I kept praying for him and saw that his heart was getting healed and he stopped crying. When God completely restored him, I was back again in Sweden. I was surprised and wondered about the experience.

After several days I had finished my meetings and went to England. I had several meetings there and was then scheduled to return to India. In the first week of being back, I bumped into the same pastor I saw in my vision. As soon as I saw him, everything I had done and seen in the spirit came to my mind. I took this pastor aside and began to ask him about what happened during the week and time I had my vision. He looked very strange at me and before he could open his mouth, I asked him if he was thinking about committing suicide. He immediately began crying very loudly, and told me that he should have been dead by now. But God saved him and protected him. I then told him how God prompted me to pray in the spirit for him as I was in Sweden. He then told me he did not know how or what had stopped him from killing himself. But I know. God used my prayers to divert the destruction of the enemy against this pastor.

Many times God takes me to pray for someone who is in need as I pray in the spirit. God has saved people from accidents and even death when people are in danger. This is one of the powerful gifts God has given us to use as promised in the Word of God. This is one of the implications the Bible refers to when it says that we are the body of Christ and Jesus is the head. If any part of the body is hurt, then the whole body is hurt with it (1 Corinthians 12:12-26).

When we stay connected to the Spirit of God, we stay connected to the source of life. We are much safer in that place. God also protects us through someone who prays in the spirit. The Holy Spirit wakes up many of us in the middle of the night or the early morning. We don't care to pray for someone who is in need at that hour. But I beg you: please do not do this! When you are tired and sleeping deeply, then suddenly wake up feeling fresh and wide awake, this is because God wants you to immediately pray for someone or something. You may not know why you are praying or what you are praying for, but you just begin by praying in tongues. The minute you begin to pray in the spirit according to God's will, the more blessing you will be to someone. God has made us watchmen. We are intercessors who do our job faithfully, bringing Heaven to earth.

Intercession birthed by the Holy Spirit can help many people who are in trouble, those who are hurt, wounded, sick, or in danger. God knows everything and always wants to help the saints (all the people who are washed by the blood of Jesus and who have Him in their hearts). God wants to protect and comfort everyone going through difficult times. The Holy Spirit will organize another who has a heart of intercession or the gift of speaking in tongues to pray for someone in a difficult situation. God will inspire them to pray in the spirit to protect them. Not only this, but evil situations can be changed into good by praying in the spirit. God may cause you to pray against the storms or against the disasters which are taking place. You know God can hear your prayers only if you are a man or woman who has a passion for other people or passion for souls.

Amos says, "Surely the Lord GOD will do nothing, but he revealeth his secret unto his servants the prophets" (Amos 3:7). Abraham interceded for Sodom and Gomorrah in Genesis 19. He asked God if there were fifty righteous people living in the city, would God still destroy it. He then asked if He would spare the city for forty righteous people, or even thirty. He finally came down to ten people. God heard his prayer and He was ready to save the city if there were only ten righteous people there—but ten could not be found. Instead God saved Lot and his family. He brought them out of Sodom and Gomorrah as judgment came upon the city and it burned.

God has given unto us a message of reconciliation:

> To wit, that God was in Christ, reconciling the world unto himself, not imputing their trespasses unto them; and hath committed unto us the word of reconciliation. Now then we are ambassadors for Christ, as though God did beseech you by us: we pray you in Christ's stead, be ye reconciled to God. For he hath made him to be sin for us, who knew no sin; that we might be made the righteousness of God in him. — 2 Corinthians 5:19-21

Standing In The Gap

Ezekiel 22:30-31 says, "And I sought for a man among them, that should make up the hedge, and stand in the gap before me for the land, that I should not destroy it: but I found none. Therefore have I poured out mine indignation upon them; I have consumed them with the fire of my wrath: their own way have I recompensed upon their heads, saith the Lord GOD." God was looking for a man who could stand in the gap between Him and the people, to intercede for them. But Ezekiel said that God couldn't find anyone. The reason there was destruction was because the intercessors failed to stand in the gap.

Another example from the time of Moses reveals the importance of standing in the gap:

> And Moses said unto Aaron, Take a censer, and put fire therein from off the altar, and put on incense, and go quickly unto the congregation, and make an atonement for them: for there is wrath gone out from the LORD; the plague is begun. And Aaron took as Moses commanded, and ran into the midst of the congregation; and, behold, the plague was begun among the people: and he put on incense, and made an atonement for the people. And he stood between the dead and the living; and the plague was stayed. — Numbers 16:46-48

The people of Israel murmured against Moses, Aaron, and even God. God was upset because of this and wanted to destroy them all. So a plague began and many of the people died. Moses commanded Aaron to take the censer filled with incense to make atonement for the people. The incense that went before God and the atonement that was made is symbolic of the prayers and the sacrifices made before God. This is what stopped the wrath of God and the plague from killing more people.

In Exodus 32 we see that because the Israelites sinned against God, He was upset and tried to destroy them. But Moses said, "Yet now, if thou wilt forgive their sin—; and if not, blot me, I pray thee, out of thy book which thou hast written" (Exodus 32:32). We can see the heart of Moses here. Even though the Israelites sinned against God, His mercy came to them because Moses stood in the gap and interceded for them.

God Delivers Peter

When the church prayed for Peter to be released from prison, God delivered him. They stood in the gap, interceding on his behalf to be released.

> Peter therefore was kept in prison: but prayer was made without ceasing of the church unto God for him. And when Herod would have brought him forth, the same night Peter was sleeping between two soldiers, bound with two chains: and the keepers before the door kept the prison. And, behold, the angel of the Lord came upon him, and a light shined in the prison: and he smote Peter

on the side, and raised him up, saying, Arise up quickly. And his chains fell off from his hands. And the angel said unto him, Gird thyself, and bind on thy sandals. And so he did. And he saith unto him, Cast thy garment about thee, and follow me. And he went out, and followed him; and wist not that it was true which was done by the angel; but thought he saw a vision. When they were past the first and the second ward, they came unto the iron gate that leadeth unto the city; which opened to them of his own accord: and they went out, and passed on through one street; and forthwith the angel departed from him. And when Peter was come to himself, he said, Now I know of a surety, that the LORD hath sent his angel, and hath delivered me out of the hand of Herod, and from all the expectation of the people of the Jews. — Acts 12:5-11

The Destruction Of The Twin Towers

God spoke to many people to intercede before planes were flown into the Twin Towers. There was a little boy, only eight or nine years old, who I met in India after this tragic event took place. As he was praying in the middle of the night, he told me about an angel who came to him and took him to Heaven. God revealed to him many different things;

but one of the things God showed him was that destruction was coming—that there were bad people who were going to blow up the Twin Towers. God showed him that many people would have to pray against this so it wouldn't happen. It was not revealed to him which towers or even which country it would be in.

But he did see the towers while watching television before they were destroyed. He tried to tell his father that these buildings were in his vision that he had seen, but his father did not believe him. Some time went by and the boy was shocked when the event of the destruction of the Twin Towers aired on the news. He told his dad, "See, these are the buildings which I told you about that would be blown up and they have been! I also heard that many will know and hear from God to pray, but I do not know or understand why this happened. Was there not enough prayer?" Only God knows that answer, but I think that it was very possible there was not enough prayer to divert the destruction.

Visitation Of Jesus During Intercession

I continued to pray during the night a few years back while in Pittsburgh. The power of the Holy Spirit increased as I continued in prayer until early in the morning. Then, when I went and laid down on my bed, continuing to pray in the spirit, I saw the roof of the bedroom open. I was lifted up through the hole and began to fly over the city of Pittsburgh. I saw the whole city lit up since it was only two or three in the morning. This lasted for a few minutes.

I suddenly accelerated and was transported to another nation where I could see many trees—like a forest. I saw tribal people as I gently landed behind some of the huts in the forest. The Holy Spirit led me to walk by the huts and then I saw a woman with her young daughter. Both of them saw me walking towards them; they were surprised and shocked to see me there. They asked me who I was. As soon as I heard them speak, the Holy Spirit inspired me to tell them, "Jesus has sent me to tell you that He loves you." I then began to explain to them about the love of Jesus, and when I repeated this, suddenly Jesus appeared standing next to them with a prayer shawl covering His face. He was holding both ends of the white and blue colors of the shawl. He slowly opened up His hands as He was looking at me with a smile. He was so beautiful! I saw His eyes were full of love and I began to cry. The women asked me why I was crying, so I responded, "Don't you see that Jesus is standing next to you? He is saying that He loves you." Then they understood the power of God's love for them. When He touched them, slowly the Holy Spirit instructed me to walk away behind the huts. As I walked behind them the Holy Spirit took me back and I was right back in my room in Pittsburgh.

Praying in tongues is a very powerful experience. The heart of Jesus is love. In the time of Jesus, two thousand years ago, He was moved with compassion for the hurting and wounded people. He healed them and touched them. Even when the leper approached Him asking if it was His will to heal him, Jesus, "Moved with compassion, put forth his hand, and touched him, and saidth unto him, I will; be thou clean. And as soon as he had spoken, immediately the leprosy departed from him, and he was cleansed" (Mark 1:41-42). The heart of God is full of love and compassion—this is the same thing He expects us to have as well. No matter what we do—sacrifice, give, and move the mountains by faith—if we don't have love, we are nothing (1 Corinthians 13). One important aspect for us to be complete in Him is to have His love flowing out of us. This love is also needful in order to effectively pray for others.

Many of you are eagerly waiting to see visions, dreams, and miracles. Unless you start praying and give yourself to God by prayer and supplication, it will be extremely difficult for you to see manifestations of the gifts of the Holy Spirit in your life. You need to pray for others who are in need and ask God to fill you with His love for other people. Begin to pray for others in the same way you pray for yourself and your own family. That kind of love and burden will begin to change the lives of people as you pray for them, delivering and healing them.

When I was filled with the Holy Spirit, I was blessed with the gift of speaking in tongues. I was eagerly waiting to see myself operating in different gifts as well, but nothing was happening. I kept asking God, "Open my eyes and show me the visions." I asked Him to use me through prophecy. Then He spoke to me and said, "Be faithful in what I have given you and I will bless you with other gifts."

So I started praying in tongues more often; being faithful with what God had given me. I started with fifteen minutes a day. I then began praying randomly at all times of the day while walking and traveling. I never had a chance to look at my watch to see how much time I was actually praying. Then I thought, "Let me see how much time I can pray in the spirit a day." After three or four days of praying for fifteen minutes a day, I increased it to a half hour a day. Then, at the end of ten days, I could pray in the spirit for an hour. There was a time before I started my ministry when I could pray for eight, ten, or even fifteen hours straight. This obviously began to open up a whole new world for me. God began to transport me into a new realm of the Kingdom. Praying this way enabled me to help bless many people.

Speaking in tongues is among the nine gifts of the Spirit, but there are diversities of tongues (1 Corinthians 12:10). There are different uses of tongues given to people in the body; and this particular gift will affect your life. You will grow strong in your faith, be edified, and connected to God in a much deeper way. Many of the supernatural gifts and experiences will be downloaded in your spirit man. It is literally going to open up your spiritual senses. You will grasp deeper things than the natural senses can provide you with. This is all done through the Holy Spirit by the gift of speaking in tongues. This is why Paul is so adamant: "and forbid not to speak with tongues" (1 Corinthians 14:39). It is a personal and foundational gift for the Christian life. The more you speak in tongues, the more the other eight gifts will begin to operate in a more marvelous and powerful way.

I have prayed for many people whom I have never met in my life. God has had me pray for many different nations, presidents, prime ministers, and actors from Hollywood. He will have us pray according to His will and in accordance with the needs of the body of Christ in different parts of the world. You will pray for help to come to others because God has kept you so you can intercede for the blessing of others—to stand in the gap. God loves everyone—but He has a special affection towards His children who obey Him.

When former President George H.W. Bush was in office, he was visiting another nation while I was in Germany. God showed me through a vision that I should pray for protection for him. The next day I saw on the news that the President had fainted, but was safe. God showed me to pray for Boris Yeltsin when he was in office, even though I didn't know anything about him. The next day on the news it was posted that he had been sick but was completely restored. God also gave me such a burden to pray for the Royal Family in England many years back. He showed me different things about them while I was praying for them. I saw a group of the Royal Family in a vision, where Prince Charles was present. I knew in my spirit that Prince Charles did not like the truth of the Word of God during that time. I felt he was involved in something else. I prayed for mercy and continued to pray for this family. I felt he needed much mercy during this time. Though I never knew what was going on, I know the prompting from God to pray for him was real.

God's Mercy Comes When You Pray

"And the Lord said, Simon, Simon, behold, Satan hath desired to have you, that he may sift you as wheat: But I have prayed for thee, that thy faith fail not: and when thou art converted, strengthen thy brethren" (Luke 22:31-32). Jesus interceded for Peter because He knew the devil was going to test him. But he was protected because of the prayer of Jesus. He had made many mistakes, but he served God faithfully to the end.

There have been many times when God has had me pray for people who are men of God that have fallen into sin. I simply pray for mercy for them; and many of their lives have been restored. Sometimes men of God have fallen into different addictions that God has revealed to me. When I share what God has shown me with these people, they become afraid, but almost always repent afterwards. God gives this gift to help people who are falling away from Him so they can be restored back into fellowship with Him.

After God had begun to excel me into His Spirit and the gifts that operate within this realm, there was an early morning some years ago when He had me in intercession. After some time I was under the power of the Holy Spirit and God took me to this nightclub where I could see some people I knew. There was a pastor who was secretly there; he was drunk and I could tell he barely had any clothes on. Though I could see him, he couldn't see me. I immediately knew of the many different kinds of sin he was involved in. I was back again and shocked I had seen those things. I didn't know how to handle this. I told some of my friends about this, asking them for wisdom, but they too were shocked and could not believe me. In less than a month, this pastor was publically exposed. I felt bad because I didn't know how to help him.

Later on I was in North East India, preaching to a big crowd of ten thousand people. A revival began the second day I was there. A large crowd came forward as I announced the altar call—they were weeping, praying, and giving their lives to Jesus. I had been praying for about a month before this meeting in Nagaland. I was still praying for it when I arrived, just before I went up to preach. God had shown me about the people there, about how many of the young people were bound. I saw in the Spirit the different people, the young people locked up with different types of addictions and sins. But as I continued to pray in the spirit, I saw them getting delivered. And so, this actually began to happen on the second day of the crusade. They wept so loud as they repented, and they began to throw away all their drugs and cigars. It is powerful to be connected with the Holy Spirit and God Himself.

First Corinthians 14:15 says, "What is it then? I will pray with the spirit, and I will pray with the understanding also: I will sing with the spirit, and I will sing with the understanding also." When we begin to pray in tongues every day, we will perfect the art of praying in the spirit. God will give us understanding about what we're praying for. Sometimes we'll be amazed to hear our own prayers in our own language. Our prayer in tongues will turn into understanding, which means we are receiving prophetic words or the interpretation of tongues. Paul says we're to ask for the interpretation if we are speaking in tongues.

But when we begin to go deeper and deeper with God, when we are full of the Holy Ghost, then we will discover differing languages coming out of our mouth. Sometimes funny sounds will come out and we'll hear ourself singing in a heavenly language with a heavenly tune, which will be very beautiful indeed. When people begin to sing in the spirit, they also dance before God at times. But if we keep singing and worshipping before God, we may end up singing the interpretation of what we had been signing in our heavenly language.

Speaking In Tongues Produces Faith

Praying in tongues will strengthen your faith. Jude writes, "But ye, beloved, building up yourselves on your most holy faith, praying in the Holy Ghost" (Jude 20). When you speak in tongues for hours on end, it can cleanse you from all your fear and replace it with tremendous faith. The Word and the Spirit always work together. Faith comes from praying in the spirit; but it also comes from hearing the Word of God: "So then faith cometh by hearing, and hearing by the word of God" (Romans 10:17).

Taking both of these Scriptures together will cause your faith to grow. In the beginning the Spirit of God was moving on the waters for many years, but there was no creation (Genesis 1). When God spoke the word, however, the Holy Spirit began to create everything. Hebrews 11:3 says, "Through faith we understand that the worlds were framed by the word of God, so that things which are seen were not made of things which do appear." If the Word and the Spirit didn't work together, then there wouldn't be any creation. So faith comes by hearing God's Word and by praying in tongues.

You will see yourself totally differently as your faith increases. You will see transformation take place because you believe God at His Word, and then you begin to do the impossible. Boldness will come inside of you and the Scriptures will be true in your life. You will be like a bold lion.

Before the crucifixion of Jesus, Peter couldn't stand for truth. He couldn't face a little girl and denied three times that he even knew Jesus. But when the Holy Spirit fell on the day of Pentecost, the same Peter who behaved so cowardly was completely transformed under the anointing of God. He stood before thousands of people and spoke the truth of God with boldness. There were about three thousand people added to the church that day. That is the type of transformation that is going to take place as you build up yourself on God's Word and the Spirit of faith.

Rest And Refreshing

The gift of tongues also brings rest and refreshing to your soul according to Isaiah 28:11-12: "For with stammering lips and another tongue will he speak to this people. To whom he said, This is the rest wherewith ye may cause the weary to rest; and this is the refreshing: yet they would not hear."

When you are physically and mentally worn out, the best thing you can do is to sing to God, worship Him, speak in tongues, and quote His Word. You will feel refreshed; joy and peace will flood into you. You will experience rest like never before. It is important for us to have rest and peace while being in this confused world. The Holy Spirit can produce this special refreshing and rest in our life.

I become physically tired after traveling for many hours, doing different types of physical work, or walking for many miles. When I meditate on God's Word as well as speak in tongues under the anointing, though I feel like fainting, suddenly God lifts me up with freshness and strength. After a hard day of working and being occupied in different activities, I am physically worn out and stressed. The only thing I think about is going to bed. However, I try to pray in the spirit and ask God to fill me with His anointing. I start to speak in tongues for only a few minutes, but then end up praying in the spirit for an hour or two because it totally refreshes me. There are some days I only get about two hours of sleep, but God gives me special strength so that

I can do all things through Him and be ready for the work that is ahead of me that day. You should always remember that God will fulfill His Word, when you believe and quote it during your prayer time (speaking in tongues). You can quote things like: "The Lord is my strength. Not I but Christ liveth in me (Galatians 2:20)." God refreshes me, fills me with His peace, and strengthens me every time I do this.

You can also study about the importance of rest and refreshing in the life of Jesus. Many times He would pray all through the night, being refreshed and healthy the following day as He preached and healed the people. Of course He took a little nap in the boat during the storm too. But we see in His life that He was a very busy man. Since we are a new creation in God, His strength can enable us to do many things supernaturally, even more than our mind can think, just like Jesus.

After Samson killed a thousand men with a donkey's jawbone, he was tired, faint, and exhausted. God supernaturally created a fountain he could drink from when he cried out to the Lord. He was refreshed and renewed as he drank the water, which is a symbol of the Holy Spirit. Judges 15:15-20 (ESV) adds:

And he found a fresh jawbone of a donkey, and put out his hand and took it, and with it he struck 1,000 men. And Samson said,
"With the jawbone of a donkey,
heaps upon heaps,
with the jawbone of a donkey
have I struck down a thousand men."
As soon as he had finished speaking, he threw away the jawbone out of his hand. And that place was called Ramath-lehi.
And he was very thirsty, and he called upon the LORD and said, "You have granted this great salvation by the hand of your servant, and shall I now die of thirst and fall into the hands of the uncircumcised?" And God split open the hollow place that is at Lehi, and water came out from it. And when he drank, his spirit returned, and he revived. Therefore the name of it was called En-hakkore; it is at Lehi to this day. And he judged Israel in the days of the Philistines twenty years.

Through God's Spirit we can do more than normal people because He gives us the energy needed to do His work. Many times I am surprised at how God has restored my strength and given me the extra ability to do more for Him.

We are friends with an anointed, beautiful, elderly couple who are always smiling and full of the Holy Ghost. They recently went on their vacation, and while coming back God gave this man divine strength to safely drive home, eleven hours non-stop! He is eighty-six years old!

It is said of God:

> He giveth power to the faint; and to them that have no might he increaseth strength. Even the youths shall faint and be weary, and the young men shall utterly fall: But they that wait upon the LORD shall renew their strength; they shall mount up with wings as eagles; they shall run, and not be weary; and they shall walk, and not faint. — Isaiah 40:29-31

This Scripture is for all of us—both young and old. Even the young men will faint, but not those who wait on God. Whoever stays in His presence and believes on His Word can receive special strength from Him. They will fly like an eagle and never be weary—they will be strong.

You will be able to do more, even beyond your natural ability, with the strength God provides. I have personally experienced this over and over throughout my life. Many men and women of God have experienced this supernatural power of God as well. I have used my body more than my abilities would naturally allow because of the strength of God. My friends were surprised to see how I could do this.

I encourage you to pray in the spirit by asking God to fill you with more of His anointing and His Word. You can do the same things Jesus did because He dwells within you — the very same things that Moses, Abraham, and Paul did.

Chapter 21

The Glory Of God

Be glad then, ye children of Zion, and rejoice in the LORD your God: for he hath given you the former rain moderately, and he will cause to come down for you the rain, the former rain, and the latter rain in the first month. And the floors shall be full of wheat, and the fats shall overflow with wine and oil. And I will restore to you the years that the locust hath eaten, the cankerworm, and the caterpiller, and the palmerworm, my great army which I sent among you. — Joel 2:23-25

God promises in Joel that when the former rain comes, He will begin to correct, prepare, and revive us before the coming of the latter rain. He prospers us by restoring to us what the enemy has stolen for many years. The latter rain speaks of the greater glory and presence of God coming to the people.

Ezekiel shared his vision about a man measuring a river in Ezekiel 47:3-10. The man with the measuring rod measured the water, and each time he measured it, the water level had increased—from ankle deep, to knee deep, to waist deep, eventually turning into a mighty river that couldn't be walked through. The peculiar part of this river was that it had the character for healing and gave life. Wherever the river flowed, there was healing and life sprang up. Not only that, but wherever this water was, there was a multitude of fish.

This river is a prophetic symbol of the Holy Spirit. How this river increased is the way the glory of God can be increased in our lives. Jesus said that anyone who comes to Him and drinks, "out of his belly shall flow rivers of living water" (John 7:38). Wherever the Holy Spirit moves with the double portion anointing, mighty things happen. More souls will be won and more people will be healed.

The power and presence of the Holy Spirit we're talking about can move everywhere, even into the nations. Many of us have experienced ankle deep, knee deep, or waist deep in the Holy Spirit. But my challenge to you is this: go deeper with the Holy Spirit. Let go of all control and let the Holy Spirit have control of your life. He wants you to be submerged in His presence, using you to your fullest potential and His greatest glory.

CHAPTER 22

Transported

Jesus often talked about the Kingdom of God. Throughout the Gospels and many of His parables, Jesus talked about what the Kingdom of God was like and how we can recognize it. Jesus told us to "seek ye first the kingdom of God, and his righteousness; and all these things shall be added unto you" (Matthew 6:33). He taught us to pray, "Thy kingdom come. Thy will be done in earth, as it is in heaven" (Matthew 6:10). And He told the disciples, "And as ye go, preach, saying, The kingdom of heaven is at hand. Heal the sick, cleanse the lepers, raise the dead, cast out devils: freely ye have received, freely give" (Matthew 10:7-8). This recognition of the Kingdom was also apparent in His disciples. So it is no wonder then that when Philip preached, prayed for sick, and cast out demons, there was such joy that came into that city (Acts 8:8).

Paul thought the Kingdom of God was important too. He wrote to the Ephesians: "And hath raised us up together, and made us sit together in heavenly places in Christ Jesus" (Ephesians 2:6). Though we live in the natural world, our spirit man is created in the image of God. We live on the earth with our natural bodies, but in the spirit we can be seated in heavenly places in Christ Jesus. To put it another way: we live in another realm while living in the present one.

Sometimes during worship at church, God's presence begins to come. As this happens I have seen angels joining us in worship. Some people have even reported that they have seen angels playing instruments while worshipping.

While worshipping God by myself in my room, His presence filled my room like a cloud. Two angels suddenly appeared and one of them spoke to me, giving me direction for my life. When we are in His presence and His glory, we are already transported into another realm. The more time we spend in His presence, the more we realize how things are going to change. God will begin to show us the deeper things of Heaven, which we have not experienced before.

That is why we need to be transported into the spiritual realm, where we can believe and catch what God is trying to tell us. Faith is one of the steps that will take us into that realm—the realm of God. When we believe God for the impossible to become possible, it will help us live in another dimension so we can receive from God and see the impossible become a reality. It is in this realm where we tap into those miracles, healings, and hidden treasures which reserved in Heaven for us.

God promises in Haggai 2:8-9, "The silver is mine, and the gold is mine, saith the LORD of hosts. The glory of this latter house shall be greater than the former, saith the LORD of hosts: and in this place will I give peace, saith the LORD of hosts." The glory of God will be doubled in the latter days. More of His presence and glory will be poured out in the latter days than was poured out in the former days. And when there is more of the presence of God, there are more creative miracles.

The glory will not come without God being present. So if we are going to experience greater glory, then that means we are experiencing greater intimacy with God. There is always acceleration in the glory realm. Things happen very fast. This is why Amos writes, "Behold, the days come, saith the

LORD, that the plowman shall overtake the reaper, and the treader of grapes him that soweth seed; and the mountains shall drop sweet wine, and all the hills shall melt" (Amos 9:13). By the time the person sowing seed is finished, the harvest will have already come. Things happen fast while in the glory realm! The time between sowing and reaping will be overlapped in the realm of God's glory.

Jonah realized that God could cause things to happen one day, and the very next day they were gone. "And the LORD God prepared a gourd, and made it to come up over Jonah, that it might be a shadow over his head, to deliver him from his grief. So Jonah was exceedingly glad of the gourd. But God prepared a worm when the morning rose the next day, and it smote the gourd that it withered" (Jonah 4:6-7). Notice how quickly God can do something in our life. When we learn to stay in His glory, we will be in a different zone—a zone of miracles and a zone of acceleration. God is doing great things these days; and He's doing them quickly.

Jesus told His disciples about the need for the harvest to be ready: "Say not ye, There are yet four months, and then cometh harvest? behold, I say unto you, Lift up your eyes, and look on the fields; for they are white already to harvest" (John 4:35). It is my desire for you to truly understand this Scripture. Jesus is trying to teach His disciples something here. While showing them the wheat field, which naturally takes four months for it to come to harvest, He is making a spiritual point. If they could see with their eyes of the spirit they would understand that the harvest was ripe—it was ready now! They didn't have to wait long—it was happening then.

Since "faith is" (Hebrews 11:1), then that means if we have spiritual eyes of faith by dwelling in His glory, then the future promises can happen in the present. Jesus is the same yesterday, today, and forever. He knows the future. He is able to bring the future into the present. When Jesus saw His disciples struggling in the boat, He went to them walking on the water. The disciples were afraid until Jesus said, "It is I; be not afraid" (John 6:17-21). It was only then that they received Jesus into their boat. Then they immediately reached the other side. They were transported to the shore—they didn't have to paddle to get to the shore.

Lazarus had been dead a few days by the time Jesus showed up (John 11:21-26, 40-44). Martha talked to Him once He arrived, telling Him that if He had been there, Lazarus wouldn't have died. But Jesus simply told her that her brother would rise again. Martha knew that at the resurrection he would rise again, but she was speaking about the present moment, not a future resurrection. Then "Jesus said unto her, I am the resurrection, and the life: he that believeth in me, though he were dead, yet shall he live" (John 11:25). Jesus was trying to teach Martha an important point because she was thinking that her brother was going to rise in the time of the resurrection—the future. He was trying to tell her, "I know what can happen in the future for your brother. But I can bring the future miracle into the present." Then we see how Jesus raised Lazarus with such a great demonstration of His power. And then "Jesus saith unto [Martha], Said I not unto thee, that, if thou wouldest believe, thou shouldest see the glory of God?" Praise God for our God! He is the God of miracles. He can do the things instantly!

You will be altogether a different person when you are touched by the glory of God. The glory strengthens your spirit man, but it also refreshes and brings life to your physical body. Moses stayed in the glory of God and shone when he came out. He died when he was one hundred and twenty, but his eyesight was still perfect. God's promise was true: "But they that wait upon the LORD shall renew their strength" (Isaiah 40:31).

There are present day testimonies of how God multiplied money when the glory of God was present. Gold, silver, diamonds, rubies, and other precious stones appeared when His glory showed up. These things are happening all around the world today. It is just like in Heaven. There is always joy, happiness, and abundance in Heaven. There is no sickness in Heaven. Everything we need is there in abundance. When you pray for Heaven to come down to earth, just like Jesus taught us to do ("Thy kingdom come. Thy will be done in earth, as it is in heaven"), then God and His angels show up, bringing all their blessings with them.

When the cloud of glory appeared in the Old Testament, God would pour out manna for the people to eat. God provided everything the Israelites would need throughout their forty years of wilderness wanderings. Even their shoes and clothes didn't wear out.

Some people have a problem believing that God can pour out His blessings through all these miracles of money multiplying and gemstones appearing. If Jesus multiplied five loaves and two fishes to feed five thousand people, He surely can multiply money also. When the disciples couldn't catch fish during the night, with one word of Jesus they caught many fish just by casting their nets on the other side of the boat. When Jesus needed to pay the tax, He asked one of His disciples to go and catch a fish because there would be enough money in the mouth of the fish to pay His and Peter's tax. If the disciples found money in the fish's mouth, why can't you find money in your house or in church?

Many years ago, after I was filled with the Holy Spirit but not in the ministry yet, I believed God for greater things. There was a time I absolutely didn't have any money at all. I checked everywhere I knew, in my pockets and many times in my closet, but there was nothing. I needed bus money to get to my college class. So I simply prayed and said to God, "You are my Provider." Then I spent some time praising Him during my ten-minute walk to catch my bus. Even though I didn't have any money, I was still walking towards the bus station. But my mind was thinking about something else. I suddenly, without thinking, put my hand into my pocket and felt something. When I took it out, there was a brand new currency note. Since I only needed a few coins for my bus ride, I had enough money for my breakfast as well as for the bus.

When I got to the restaurant for my breakfast, one of my old friends was there, happy to see me. He told me that he wanted to pay for my breakfast. Not only did he pay for my breakfast, but he also paid for my bus ticket as well. I still had that brand new currency note in my pocket. Since God had provided for me that morning, I wanted to be a blessing to others, so I gave the currency note to someone. The same evening one of my relatives met me and was so happy to see me. He also gave me another sixty rupees. In those days, that was a lot of currency. I praised God for each time He provided for me.

Another time when my family was coming back from Germany, we landed in Bangalore, India. We only had six hundred Euros on us. We had to spend about two hundred there as we traveled to Hubli. We were in need of some more money—we only had about four hundred Euros left. But when we looked at it and recounted it, we still had six hundred Euros! Praise God for the multiplication of money!

There was another time I had only forty dollars in my pocket while I was in Pittsburgh, Pennsylvania. While going to buy an item from Wal-Mart, I knew the item cost around forty dollars. When I came to the counter to pay, the bill was $40.50. I was holding the two $20 bills in my hand, while looking for change in my pocket with the other hand. While standing there, someone passing by happened to bump into me. I almost dropped the forty dollars in my hand because of this. But to my surprise, when I looked again at the money in my hand, there were three $20 bills there! I was so shocked and surprised. I paid for my item and left.

When I shared some of the ways God has provided for me with my sister in India, it created faith within her to believe God for finances too. She only had two hundred rupees in her closet. When an evangelist came to her house, she felt like she was supposed to give him one hundred of those rupees. She knew she had obeyed God, but was still feeling kind of sad because she only had one hundred left. Eventually she needed some more money, so when she went to get the one hundred rupee note, and to her shock it wasn't one hundred any more, but it was a one thousand rupees note!

In His presence there is fullness of joy. God wants to bless us. He knows our needs. The longer you stay in His glory and presence, the more you will continue to see His miracles.

A few years ago, when I was not yet married, I went to preach in Sweden. One of my Swedish friends hosted me in his house; he was not married either. I was spending a lot of time praying and worshipping God. One evening he came home with such joy and said that his company gave him three times more money that month as a bonus! That had never happened before. So the next day he needed to buy a tire for his car and went to somebody selling tires. After he bought one tire, the guy gave him the other three tires for free. My friend was extremely happy and said that because I was bringing the presence of God into his house, God was blessing him. He told his other Swedish friends, who were also friends of mine. They asked me to come to their houses too. So I went and prayed, "Lord, bless their house, too." The very next day the aunt of my friend's wife, who was a single lady, called her and said, "I have so much money I don't know what to do with it. I want to give you ten thousand Swedish kroners." My friends were very happy to receive that blessing.

God taught me to build my relationship with Him as my Father, and that helped me stay in His glory much more. Sometimes I stand up, look at Him, and talk to Him while I'm worshipping. Other times I see His glory like a cloud appearing in my room. It is so awesome to have these experiences with Him! When His presence is so near, there is such joy and ecstasy. It is difficult to explain it. I feel so fresh and have twice as much strength in the middle of the night or early in the morning because of His presence. During that time, if I have any requests, I tell Him what they are and

He immediately grants them. There have been a couple of times when my room had very little light in it, but suddenly the entire room brightens up with a bright light. When I am experiencing this kind of the presence of God, powerful things happen. Many times when the weather channel says that it is going to be raining, snowing, or lightning, I simply ask God to change the weather and God has answered me many times. It's amazing and true!

I want to suggest one last thing for you: if you are in a service and find the presence of God to be strong there, begin to ask God to grant your requests as well as you know how, sowing your money into the Kingdom of God. When His glory is there, it will be multiplied back to you almost immediately. May God bless you and fill you with His presence and glory.

Conclusion

Throughout this book I've been sharing about how powerful it is to understand that we were created in the image of God. The Holy Spirit and His Word help us grow in our faith, from one degree of glory to the next.

Take a moment and picture the creation of God—how God created Adam in His image. Adam and Eve living in God's glory must have been wonderful and extremely powerful. Adam came from God and he was completely soaked in God's glory. There was nothing lacking and they possessed all things in abundance. Adam was part of God. He had DNA from God.

When Adam sinned against God, he was cut off from His presence. The sin came in between Adam and God, and all of the sudden he couldn't walk like God any more; his relationship was cut off. There was no godly generation afterwards that walked with God in the same way Adam had done before the Fall. He lost his dominion; but more than that he lost the presence of God. The whole human race has been struggling under the dominion of sin until now. Praise God for Jesus and His shed blood. It is the blood of Jesus that makes us one again.

Now that we have been joined to Christ, we are one spirit with him: "But he that is joined unto the Lord is one spirit" (1 Corinthians 6:17). We are able to get back the DNA of God through the shed blood of Jesus. We are restored as soon as the blood of Jesus washes us and the Spirit of God fills us—the image of God is re-created within us. It is time to begin growing in His nature and His glory.

God brings us more and more into His glory so that there will be transformation and change. The Bible puts it this way: "Now the Lord is that Spirit: and where the Spirit of the Lord is, there is liberty. But we all, with open face beholding as in a glass the glory of the Lord, are changed into the same image from glory to glory, even as by the Spirit of the Lord" (2 Corinthians 3:17-18). We can begin to walk like God again, having close fellowship with Him. We are one with Him once again in Christ—just like Adam before the Fall.

In the Old Testament tabernacle, the blood was offered once a year on the Ark of the Covenant, located within the holy of holies. And when this blood was sprinkled upon the mercy seat, the glory of God would come down and cover the ark. In the same way, when the blood of Jesus washes us, then the Holy Spirit descends on us in glory because we are His temple. Our spirit longs to stay in His glory at all times so that we can become like Him and continually behold His face. Whatever the Father does, we can also do as well.

After praying many hours some years ago, I lied down on my bed. I saw a burning lamp on the wall. As I was looking at it, it began to come towards me. It came through my feet and went right through my body. It was a powerful experience. From that moment on I was a completely different person. Not only that, but many miracles began to happen after that experience too. It is God's desire to baptize each and every one of you with the Holy Ghost and fire. It is going to be a powerful, life-changing experience. So stay in His glory and continue to build up your relationship with the Father.

You can't build your relationship with Father God without faith. You can't please Him without it. For you to walk in faith, you need to have the Word of God and continually pray in the spirit. This is why it's so important to be full of the power of God and build your foundation on the Word of God.

We are living in days when God is pouring out His glory on all people. The Bible gives many examples of God's glory coming into contact with His people. Ezekiel speaks much about the glory of God while Moses gives us a visible demonstration of abiding in God's glory:

> And he said, My presence shall go with thee, and I will give thee rest. And he said unto him, If thy presence go not with me, carry us not up hence. For wherein shall it be known here that I and thy people have found grace in thy sight? is it not in that thou goest with us? so shall we be separated, I and thy people, from all the people that are upon the face of the earth. And the LORD said unto Moses, I will do this thing also that thou hast spoken: for thou hast found grace in my sight, and I know thee by name. And he said, I beseech thee, shew me thy glory. And he said, I will make all my goodness pass before thee, and I will proclaim the name of the LORD before thee; and will be gracious to whom I will be gracious, and will shew mercy on whom I will shew mercy. And he said, Thou canst not see my face: for there shall no man

see me, and live. And the LORD said, Behold, there is a place by me, and thou shalt stand upon a rock: And it shall come to pass, while my glory passeth by, that I will put thee in a clift of the rock, and will cover thee with my hand while I pass by: And I will take away mine hand, and thou shalt see my back parts: but my face shall not be seen. — Exodus 33:14-23

It was his desire to be with God and to see Him in all His glory. No wonder his life was so extraordinary.

I pray that the Holy Spirit will fill you with His glory, cause you to walk with Him, and make you see Him face to face. As you read the Bible day and night (Joshua 1:7-9) and pray in the spirit without ceasing, let His glory reveal all the hidden treasures for you as you walk with Him.

Jesus, impart to them every gift of the Holy Spirit. Bring nations to You. These are the people who are hungry. I pray You would fill them as much as they need. In Jesus' name I pray, amen! All glory to God!

Ministry Contact Information

Latter Glory Ministries
Founder, Suri Devaraj
contact@latterglory.org
www.latterglory.org

CPSIA information can be obtained at www.ICGtesting.com
Printed in the USA
BVOW012119050112
279827BV00002B/7/P